Jacob of Sarug's Homilies on Paul

Texts from Christian Late Antiquity

61

TeCLA (Texts from Christian Late Antiquity) is a series presenting ancient Christian texts both in their original languages and with accompanying contemporary English translations.

Jacob of Sarug's Homilies on Paul

On the Conversion of the Apostle Paul
and a Second Homily on Paul the Apostle

Translation and Introduction by

Raju Parakkott

Edited with Notes by

Mary T. Hansbury

2021

Gorgias Press LLC, 954 River Road, Piscataway, NJ, 08854, USA

www.gorgiaspress.com

Copyright © 2021 by Gorgias Press LLC

All rights reserved under International and Pan-American Copyright Conventions. No part of this publication may be reproduced, stored in a retrieval system or transmitted in any form or by any means, electronic, mechanical, photocopying, recording, scanning or otherwise without the prior written permission of Gorgias Press LLC.

2021

ISBN 978-1-4632-4273-2   ISSN 1935-6846

Library of Congress Cataloging-in-Publication Data

A Cataloging-in-Publication Record is available from the Library of Congress.

Printed in the United States of America

TABLE OF CONTENTS

Table of Contents v
Introduction 1
   Outline 1
   Summary 3
      The Conversion of the Apostle Paul [#61] 3
      A Second Homily on Paul the Apostle [#62] 4
Text and Translation 5
Homily 61: The Conversion of the Apostle Paul 6
   Strategems through which Jesus won the world 6
   The changes that Jesus effected on Paul 8
   The misunderstandings of Paul about Jesus Christ 10
   Paul as persecutor 16
   The Light that shone upon Paul 22
   Light of Gospel 24
   Paul speaks to Jesus 28
   Jesus speaks to Paul 38
   The dialogue between Jewish priests and Paul 44
   Dialogue between Jesus and Ananias 50
   The encounter between Paul and Ananias 54
   Jesus is sole role model of Jesus 56
   Cross and Paul 62
Homily 62: A Second Homily on Paul the Apostle 68
   Reason for writing a second mimro on St Paul the Apostle .. 68
   Commentary of Gal. 6:17 "for I carry the marks of Jesus
      branded on my body." 70
   Humility of Paul 72
   Commentary of Gal.6:17 "For I decided to know nothing
      among you except Jesus Christ, and Him crucified." 76
   Commentary of I Cor.4:9 "…we have become a spectacle
      to the people and to angels." 80

Commentary of Col. I:24 "I am filling up what is lacking in all the sufferings of Christ in body for the sake of the Church which is His body." 84
Commentary of Phil. 3:13 "I forget those things which are behind me because they are in the past and I strain forward as much as I can towards what lies ahead of me." 90
Commentary of Rom 9:3 "I have prayed that I myself were accursed for Israel's sake so that it may not be estranged from its Saviour." 98
Love of Paul for Jesus 106
Bibliography of Works Cited 113
Index 117
   Biblical References 117
   Index of Key Terms 119

INTRODUCTION

> INFORMATION ON THESE HOMILIES
> Homily Title: The Conversion of the Apostle Paul
> Source of Text: *Homiliae Selectae Mar-Jacob Sarugensis*, edited by Paul Bedjan (Paris-Leipzig: Harrassowitz, 1907), 2nd ed. Piscataway: Gorgias Press, 2006), vol. 2, pp. 717–747. [Homily 61]
>
> Homily Title: A Second Homily on Paul the Apostle
> Source of Text: *Homiliae Selectae Mar-Jacob Sarugensis*, edited by Paul Bedjan (Paris-Leipzig: Harrassowitz, 1907), 2nd ed. Piscataway: Gorgias Press, 2006), vol. 2, pp. 747–769. [Homily 62]

OUTLINE

The first *mimro* of Jacob of Serugh is a dramatic representation of the events leading up to and including the conversion episode of Paul. The story Jacob relates is rooted in the account given in the Acts of the Apostles. Jacob has pondered and plumbed the depths of this narrative, presenting it afresh in a dramatic fashion. The theme of the drama is the grace of conversion; its protagonist is a clever Hebrew whose zeal for the ancient traditions of his people drives him to persecute the followers of Jesus; its villains are the Jewish priests who are anxious to eradicate a growing threat to the *status quo*. There are other characters too. Jesus is portrayed as a kind of *deus ex machina* who intervenes all of a sudden to stop the frenzy of persecution and change the antihero into a true hero. Ananias, who was commanded to open the eyes of the persecutor, is presented as both fearful and skeptical but nevertheless does what he is bidden. The apostles are depicted as simple uneducated people in need of the more polished and erudite Paul who can hold his own in debate with the religious authorities. The narrator of the drama is its author, Jacob. The narrative line of this *mimro* is interrupted by dialogues between different characters.

By inserting dialogues into the narrative account Jacob manages to highlight certain aspects of Paul's character. The spoken words of the *dramatis personae* convey more effectively than a mere recitation of events what the author wants to stress. In these interchanges Jacob shines a light on Paul's virtues and qualities.

Jacob draws on imagery and terminology in the Bible to paint his picture of Paul. Some of these include describing Paul as spectacle or show (62:123), prisoner of Christ and servant of the cross (62:31), fool for Christ (62:166), scum of the world (62:153), Israelite and son of Abraham (62:154), Hermes and insane (62:135–136), tent maker (62:139), worker of miracles and mighty deeds (62:140), murderer and restorer of youth (62:141–142), Roman and Pharisee (62:145–146), etc. In the second *mimro* the emphasis is on Paul as convert, as someone who opted to become a persecuted one for Jesus' sake. Jacob begins with an admission that he failed to complete an adequate picture of Paul in the first *mimro*, and goes on to state that he wants to make up for this deficiency by concentrating exclusively on the sufferings Paul endured for Jesus. Through this lens of suffering, the character of Paul as preacher of Christ, imitator of Christ and persecuted one for Christ is developed in the second *mimro*.

The primary motive of Jacob of Serugh in composing the two *mimre* on the Apostle Paul is to present a meditation on this biblical character who, for Jacob, is the model *par excellence* of conversion. Paul experienced a profound change in his life when he encountered the Risen Lord on the road to Damascus. He was converted. The very act of conversion cut the convert's life in two and in these *mimre* Jacob examines and explores both halves. The erstwhile persecutor of the followers of Christ became, after his conversion, a persecuted follower of Christ. He who experienced a radical reorientation in his life went on to preach the radical message of the cross, the only authentic instrument of change. Jacob goes to the heart of the Christian message in these *mimre* on Paul. Paul is a strong hero but also a weak human being, a great sinner who became a great saint. Jacob's contemplation of the conversion of Paul is ultimately a confession of the mighty deeds of God.

Jacob creatively adds to the biblical account of his hero and imagines various scenes that are found in neither the Acts of the Apostles nor the Pauline letters. Jacob's reading of scripture fires his imagination and he explores the deeper meaning of the text by expanding the narrative. The scenes he creates are non-biblical in a literal sense but very biblical in a spiritual one. Jacob, the flute of the Spirit, is attuned to the silent music of the biblical words and can sing out their glorious melodies.

Jacob based his *mimre* on the Apostle Paul, on the biblical accounts given in both the Acts of the Apostles and in the Apostle's own letters. While there is nothing contrary to the biblical presentation in both *mimre*, there is an imaginative expansion of the narrative. This is not a betrayal of the text. Rather it is the work of Jacob's poetic genius whose deep insight into the biblical account allows him to creatively express its spiritual meaning. Jacob was possessed of a gentle and kind spirit and he eschewed all doctrinal polemics. His gentleness and humility rendered him acceptable to all and everyone. In these *mimre* he does not attempt to present controversial theological ideas about the Apostle Paul, but presents him as a model of Christian life and as a model of hope. Here is a sinner who by the grace of God was made a great saint and a 'chosen vessel'. In praising Paul he is praising the work of grace which is possible for all. The Lord who is mighty did great things for Paul. As a bishop, Jacob is preaching the same message to each of his flock. The *mimre* are no mere encomium but a pastoral message on the boundless love of God.

Summary

The Conversion of the Apostle Paul [#61]

Stratagems through which Jesus won the world (1–22)

Changes that Jesus effected in Paul (23–38)

Misunderstanding of Paul about Jesus Christ (39–56)

Paradoxical titles attributed to Paul (57–74)

Reasons for inducting learned Paul among the uneducated band of Apostles (75–104)

Paul as persecutor (105–150)

The Light that shone upon Paul (151–188)

Light of the Gospel (189–224)

Paul speaks to Jesus (225–323)

Jesus speaks to Paul (324–374)

The dialogue between Jewish priests and Paul (375–432)

Dialogue between Jesus and Ananias (433–484)

The encounter between Paul and Ananias (485–510)

Jesus is sole role model of Jesus (511–564)

Cross and Paul (565–598)

A Second Homily on Paul the Apostle [#62]

Reason for writing a second mimro on St. Paul the Apostle (1–34)

Commentary of Gal. 6:17 "…for I carry the marks of Jesus branded on my body." (35–60)

Humility of Paul (61–86)

Commentary of Gal. 6:17 "For I decided to know nothing among you except Jesus Christ, and him crucified." (87–120)

Commentary of I Cor. 4:9 "…we have become a spectacle to the people and to angels." (121–174)

Commentary of Col. 1:24 "I am filling up what is lacking in all the sufferings of Christ in body for the sake of the Church which is his body." (175–222)

Commentary of Phil. 3:13 "I forget those things which are behind me because they are in the past and I strain forward as much as I can towards what lays ahead of me." (223–300)

Commentary of Rom. 9:3 "I have prayed that I myself were accursed for Israel's sake so that it may not be estranged from its savior." (301–384)

Love of Paul for Jesus (385–414)

Text and Translation

HOMILY 61: THE CONVERSION OF THE APOSTLE PAUL

STRATEGEMS THROUGH WHICH JESUS WON THE WORLD

The humility of Jesus took the whole earth captive
and without coercion He attracted the world by His preaching.
He made Crucifixion—an emblem of shame—into an heroic feat;
being greatly dishonoured, He gave honour to those who were in need.
5   By the sufferings He endured, the world was awakened to faith in Him
and by His wounds He wrested power from the powerful.
In weakness His deeds of power did swiftly run,
(yet) people did not see His glory and do Him homage.
In mockery He laid hold of the diadem of kingliness;
10   from His bruises has His glory shone out upon creation.
What to others is a cause of shame, in Him became honour;
death overwhelms all the mighty, yet by death did He become mighty.
The Crucified took for His carriage the crippling instrument of suffering
and surpassed the fiery (chariots) of kings in their swiftness.
15   At the Crucifixion He wrenched away all veneration to the gods;
He was slain and thus exposed the falsehood of all idols on this earth.
By His lowliness He humbled the mighty in their conceit
and the crowns of rulers became a footstool at His feet.
In persecuting Him, His persecutors even became subject to Him

ܡܐܡܪܐ ܣܐ

ܘܥܠ ܩܘܕܫ ܩܘܕܫܝܢ܆ ܘܐܝܟܢ ܠܚܘܕܘܗܝ
ܡܢ ܪܒ ܟܘܡܪܐ ܡܬܥܠ.

1 ܡܫܟܢܙܒܢܐ ܘܬܩܢܗ ܪܙܐ ܠܐܪܙܐ ܫܟܢܗ܆
   ܗܘܠܐ ܕܗܘܝܢ ܒܓܘܗ ܠܚܟܡܐ ܕܚܙܝܘܗܝ.
   ܕܪܡܫܘܬܐ ܐܝܬ ܘܫܡܫܐ ܕܟܒܪ ܢܪܝܡܐ:
   ܚܕܐ ܘܠܐ ܕܟܝܢ ܬܖ̈ܝܢ ܐܬܖ̈ܘܢ ܕܒܡܣܝܢ ܗܘܘ.
5 ܚܨܦܐ ܘܡܣܟܐ ܐܝܠܝܢ ܠܟܗܢܐ ܘܒܗܢ ܡܗ.
   ܘܚܨܦܬܢܘܬܐ ܥܒܕܐ ܐܣܝܪܐ ܗܝ ܟܣܝܬܐ.
   ܟܨܝܘ̈ܬܐ ܘܗܠܝܢ ܩܘܕܫܝ̈ܗܘܢ ܡܢܟܐܝܬ܆
   ܠܐ ܡܬܚܣܠܗ ܣܘܓܐܐ ܕܢܩܘܡ ܕܐܢ ܘܢܨܐ ܒܗ.
   ܟܝ ܡܠܐܟ̈ܐ ܐܕܘܪ ܠܐܝܠ ܕܡܪ̈ܘܬܐ.
10 ܘܦܢ ܚܘܡܗ ܐܪܙܘ̈ܗܝ ܗܘܠܚܗ ܪܒܐ ܚܬܝܟܐ.
   ܚܟܡܗ ܒܐܝܣܪܐܝܠ ܡܪܗܓܪܢ ܒܗ ܐܠܐ ܐܢ ܗܘ.
   ܡܪܐ ܘܦܫܩܐ ܗܘ ܘܩܠ ܚܨ̈ܢܬܪܐ ܘܟܗ ܐܠܚܩܪ.
   ܪܐܙܐ ܥܒܝܠ ܟܗ ܘܩܘܪܐ ܪܒܚܝܨܐ ܘܡܥܠܐ ܪܒܐ.
   ܘܐܢܘܗܝ ܠܚܝܠܘ̈ܗܝ ܚܬܢܐ ܘܡܗܬܚܐ ܘܡܬܟܬܟܘܗܝ.
15 ܕܪܡܫܘܬܐ ܥܒܕܐ ܗܬܒܝܐ ܡܢ ܐܟܕܬܐ.
   ܥܝܗܝܐ ܘܡܟܢܗܐ ܚܕܡܬܐ ܘܐܘܕܐ ܘܪܟܥܐ ܐܢܘܢ.
   ܕܡܫܟܢܙܒܢܐ ܥܩܠ ܪܗܡܐ ܘܟܖ̈ܝܢܝ ܗܘܘ.
   ܗܘܘ ܐܦܢܐ ܘܡܟܬܦܘܢܐ ܩܘܕܡܐ ܠܬܝܖ̈ܟܘܗܝ.
   ܕܙܘܦܘܬܐ ܐܘ ܙܘܘܕܐ ܐܗܠܚܟܒܗ ܗܘܘ.

20 so that, without compulsion, they might accept sufferings for His sake.
By His infirmity He instructed his enemies,
so that they might become His friends and even die for Him.

THE CHANGES THAT JESUS EFFECTED ON PAUL

See! By His teaching He made the persecutor[1] into a persecuted one[2]
and the insolent one into the chosen vessel[3] of His proclamation.
25 Through Saul, the mattock,[4] who set out to uproot the churches,
He laid the foundations[5] of faith for the whole world.
He made the demolisher the architect[6] of His building,[7]
He laid the foundation upon which all true ones will construct.
The wonder is that someone can be praised by his foes
30 and that even his enemies defend his innocence.
The testimony of friends, even though trustworthy, is insufficient,
so that He enlisted His enemy to become a witness of His proclamation.
He who was full of murderous rage[8] towards the disciples
was the one He appointed to defend them, His true ones.

---

[1] Acts 9:4; 22:7; 26:14.
[2] 2 Cor. 11:23–28; Acts 16:19–24; Acts 23:23–24:27; Acts 28:16–31.
[3] Acts 9:15.
[4] 1 Sam. 13:20; 1 Sam. 13:21.
[5] 1 Cor. 3:10.
[6] 1 Cor. 3:10.
[7] 1 Cor. 3:9.
[8] Acts 26:10.

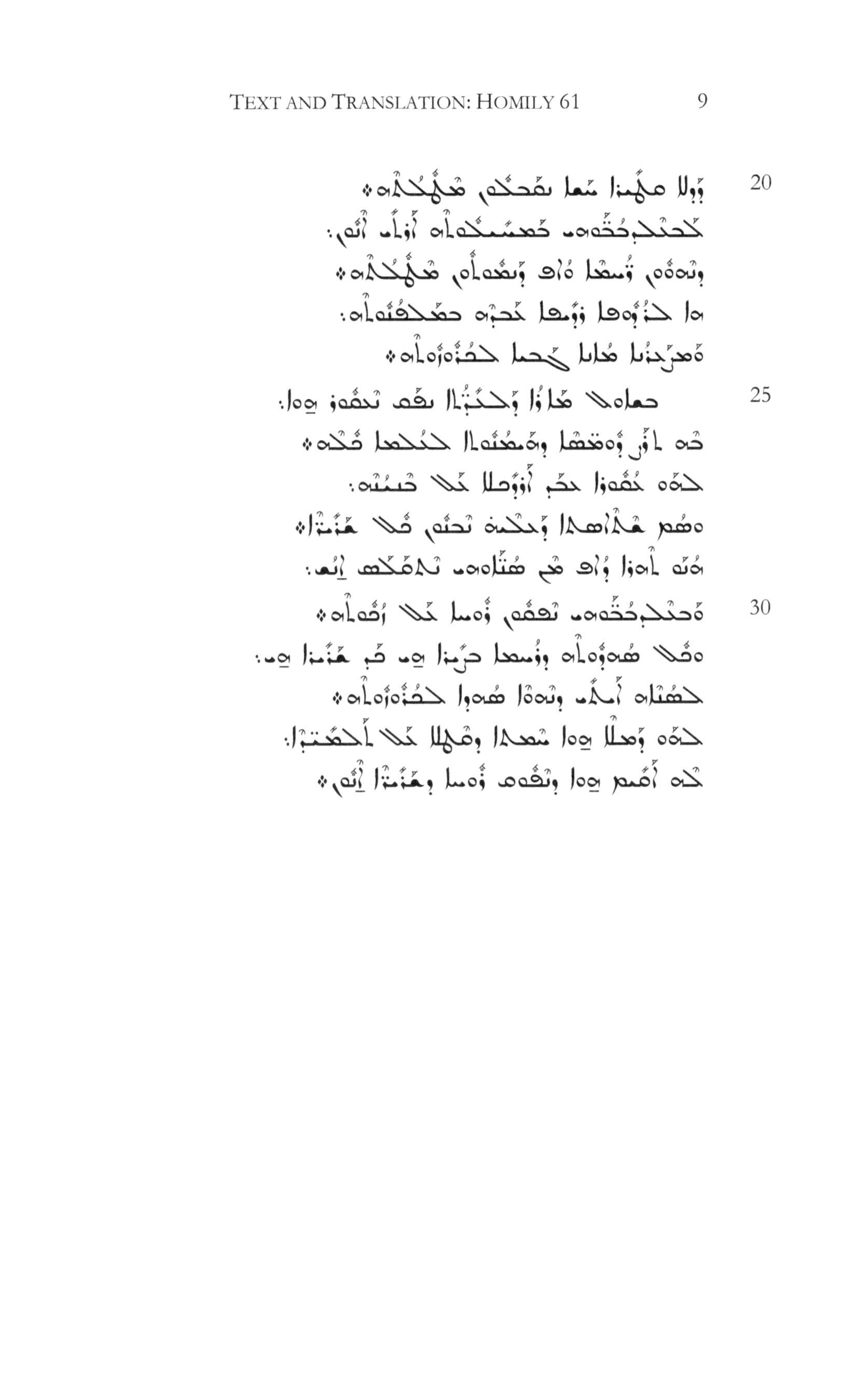

35 The man who was dragging off[9] (to prison) men and women because of Jesus,
was the very one He caused to be dragged off on account of His teaching.
Wisely He hunted the hawk[10] and turned it into a dove,[11]
showing His power over even the wildest of creatures.

THE MISUNDERSTANDINGS OF PAUL ABOUT JESUS CHRIST

Saul breathed threats[12] and was filled with anger against the disciples.
40 He inflicted all sorts of torments on them because of Jesus.
He had clothed himself with zeal for the Law of the house of Adonai,[13]
so that—not knowing his Son—he might persecute with authority.
In the vineyard of the Father he laboured with great effort,
not knowing that Jesus whom he was persecuting was the heir.
45 He was the watchman appointed to guard the Nation from the Gentiles;
he went in pursuit of the King not recognizing Him in disguise.
He was vigilant each day to protect the Lord of the Sabbath;
he made it clear he was all set and spied on Him (who was concealed) in different attire.
The Prince put on garments of low degree and went to check
50 whether the sentinel guarding the barricades was awake.
When the watchman saw Him in unbecoming and worthless apparel,
he chased after Him, as ever vigilant he never slept.
When he grew weary and did not overtake Him—spare us his effort!
—He, the Prince, manifested the brightness of His glory and flung Saul to the ground.

---

[9] Acts 8:3.
[10] Job 39:26; Lev. 11:13–16; Dt. 14:11–15.
[11] Mt. 10:16.
[12] Acts 9:1.
[13] Acts 22:3.

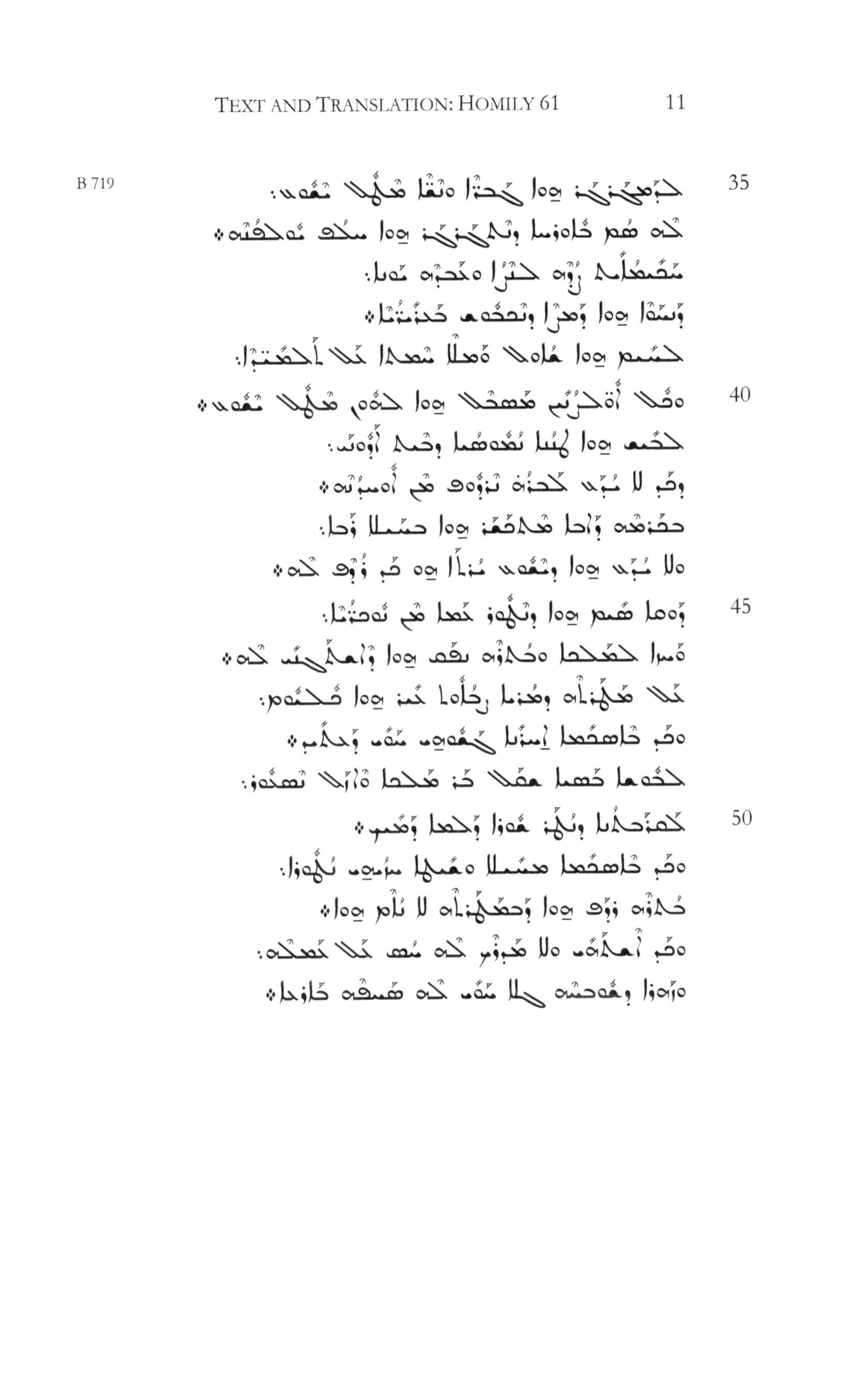

B 719

55	The brightness of the royal crown flashed on the Persecutor.
	It knocked him to the ground. The terrifying episode collared him: why was he persecuting?
	Love requires that this story be told by Love:
	listening, however intently, without love, has no effect.
	You and I will not be wearied by its length!
60	Come and rejoice! Every little detail is filled with love.
	Paul too was full of love in his preaching
	and so became a mighty champion of the Good News.
	In love, then, let me tell a story that is full of reward,
	receiving inspiration from reading the account of Paul.
65	What shall I call him? Enemy of Jesus or His friend,
	assiduous persecutor, or endlessly persecuted?
	Source of sorrow to disciples or cause of gladness to apostles,
	implacable adversary, or ardent lover?
	Eloquent scribe or mouthpiece of Judaism,
70	or harp, resonant with the music of apostleship?
	Skilled orator and interpreter of the scriptures of the house of Adonai,
	or disciple schooled in the simplicity of John?
	Wisely was he caught for the preaching of the Gospel,
	to complement the band of unschooled disciples.

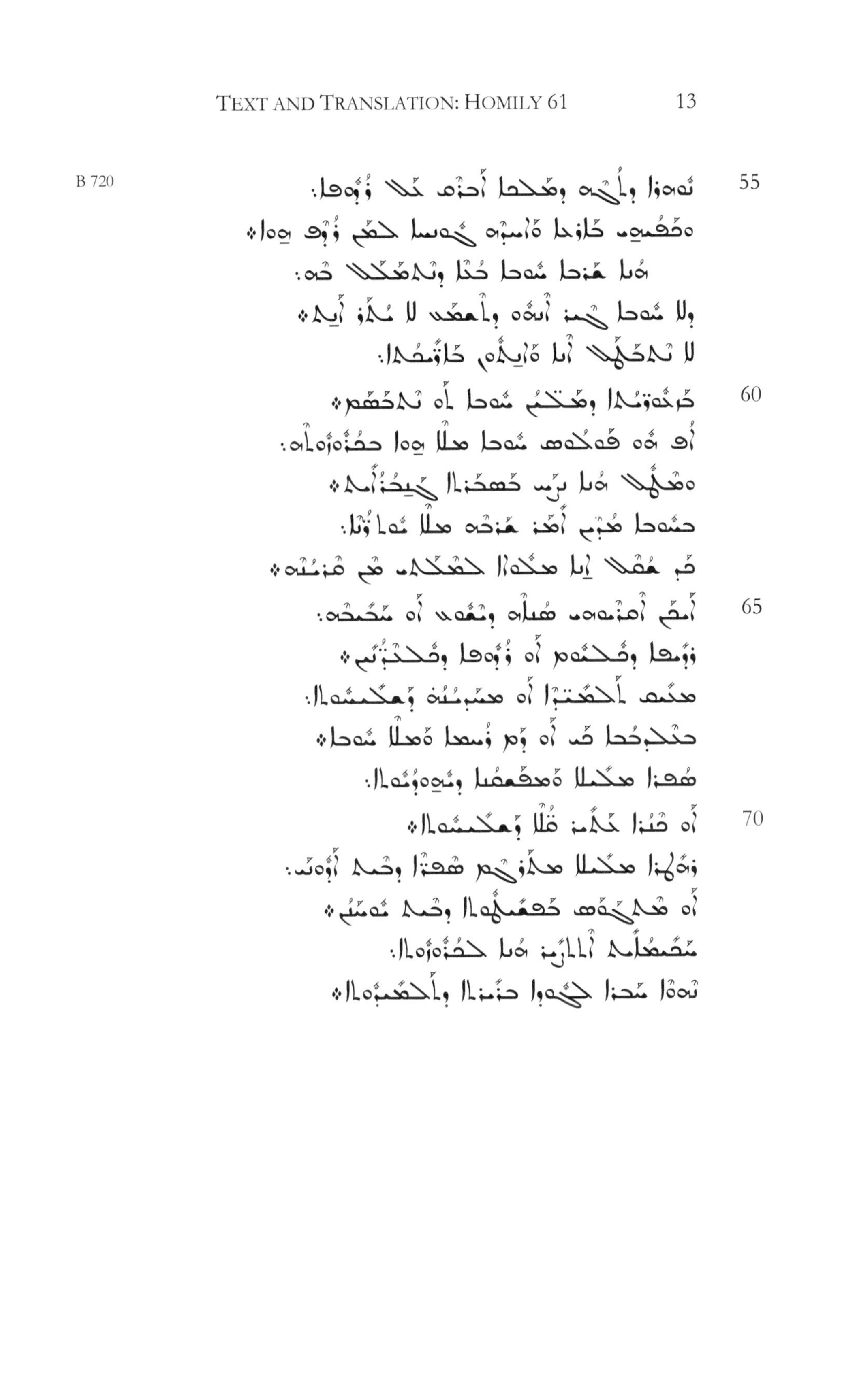

B 720

75	He chose the foolish to shame the wise;[14]
	not by clever argument but by mighty deed would He attest His teaching.
	So that the obstinate might not mock the apostles' ignorance,
	one schooled in the Law was placed in their midst.
	From inside their own house Saul grew as a thorn,[15]
80	to rebuke them through their own Law regarding the Son of the Lord.
	Simon, the chosen one, was contemptible to the scribes as a mere fisherman;
	as indeed were all the apostles who were with him, because they were ignorant men.
	For this reason He singled out Saul from among those who were learned,
	to vindicate the simple ones and prove them true.
85	So that, when they dispense with circumcision, customs and traditions,
	the Nation could not accuse them of not reading the book of Moses:
	"In their ignorance they treat with contempt the rituals of Judaism;
	they transgress the Law because they never learned it."
	It is indeed beautiful that Paul came on the scene, as we have related;
90	he, the intelligent writer, along with the unlearned apostles, will proclaim the truth.
	He who had learnt the full order of the old dispensation,
	rejected it all and boasted of the new.
	He who trained with feasts, Sabbaths and new moons,[16]
	set them aside and thereafter was just simply guided and led.

---

[14] 1 Cor. 1:27.
[15] 2 Cor. 12:7.
[16] Col. 2:16.

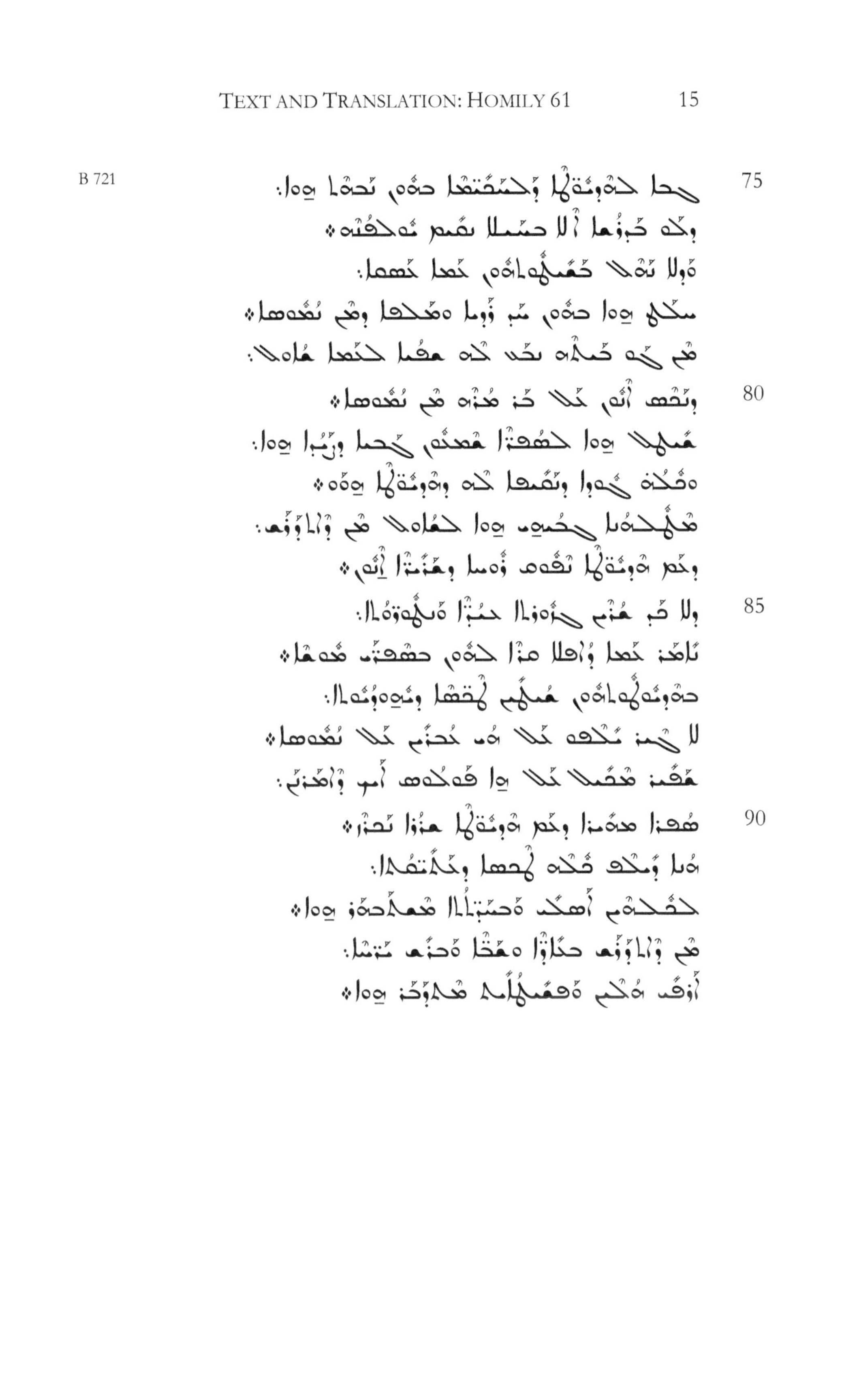

B 721

95 He who was carrying the whole burden imposed by Moses,
shrugged it off to accept the yoke of Crucifixion.
The Gospel seized this intelligent scribe to show through him
that its simplicity confounds all the intelligent ones.[17]
The skillful and learned one mingled with the simple and untaught ones,
100 without altering in any way the (essential) proclamation.
Like (Peter) the Fisherman he spoke simply
and spoke only of the Cross as, indeed, did they.
This great cause enlisted Paul as an apostle,
that the truth might be revealed to the crucifiers as the noonday sun.

Paul as Persecutor

105 He was the persecutor aptly chosen by the Lord
who took him and placed him within the circle of the apostles.
He put on zeal to take captive the disciples of the Son,
inflicting every kind of torment in His name.
He sought letters from the priestly leaders as they thirsted for blood,
110 stirring up murder against the disciples.
His anger was kindled and his fury inflamed,
as he inflicted suffering on all who professed the name of Jesus.
He was full of rage—not simply to condemn but to kill.
He was issuing threats—not simply to revile but to quench his thirst for blood.

---

[17] 1 Cor. 1:25.

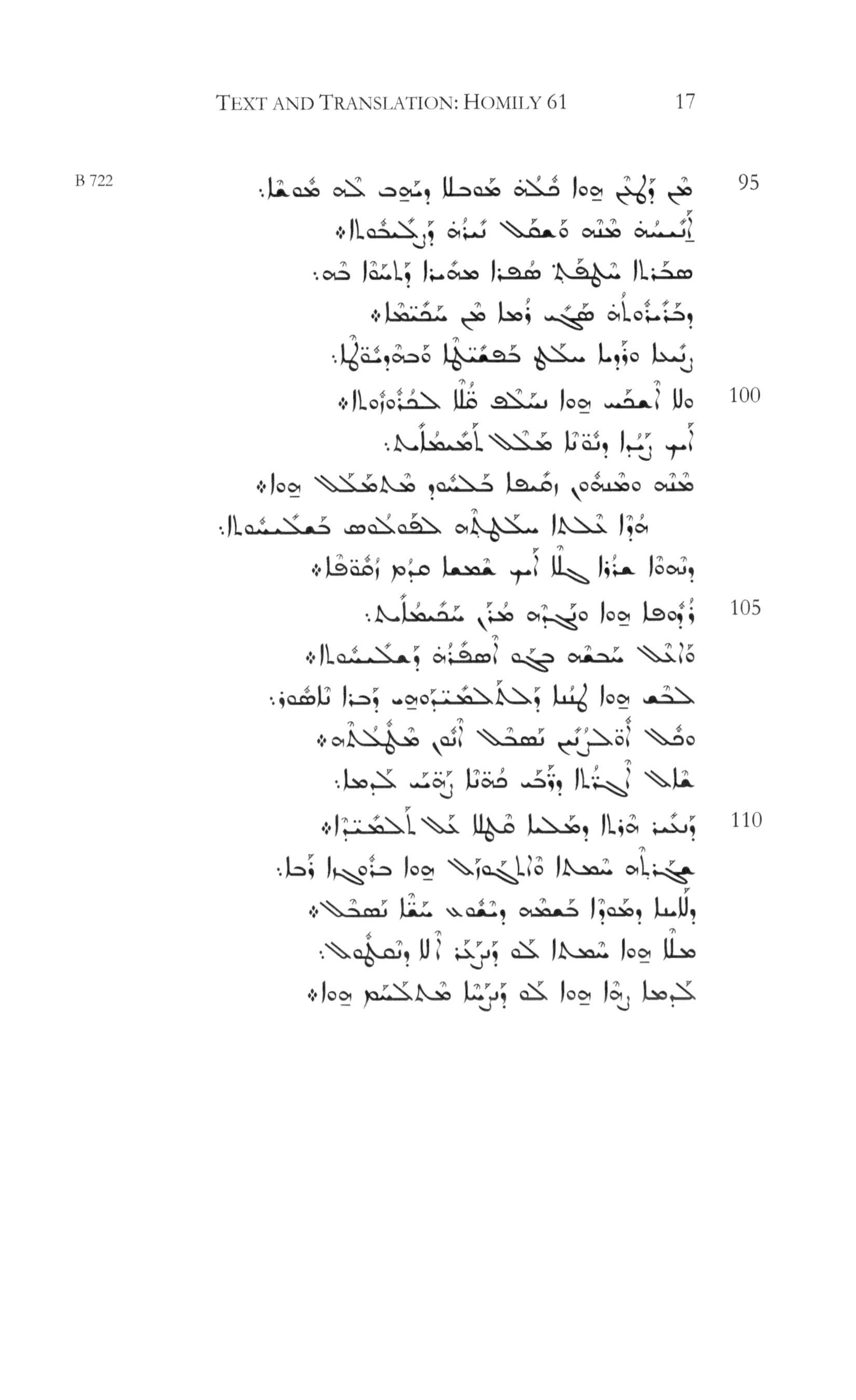

B 722

115	From the crucifiers he took up arms against the disciples.
	Their letters were mandates to murder and to inflict much suffering.
	He was supported in his pillage by priests baying for blood,
	so that he might go and brew a cup of death for the disciples.
	Astutely did Truth corner and capture him
120	that the implacable adversary might become bearer of the Good News.
	Everyone knew him as the enemy of Jesus;[18]
	later he would be called to suffer martyrdom because of his conversion.
	On the road He took him from the ranks of the persecutors and called him,
	manifesting His glory by summoning him to His side.
125	He allowed the whole world to know that Paul is His enemy,
	so that when He makes him His witness he will be trustworthy.
	He revealed Himself on the road and shrewdly pursued him
	so that he might speak of the beauties of Jesus as is His due.
	His preaching about Jesus seemed hypocrisy to his hearers
130	because only the day before he was vilifying Him harshly.
	Paul was no friend of Jesus—there was no plot between the two to deceive.
	Rather, Paul learned the truth—otherwise he would not have preached.
	He received letters (of authorization) and the whole community took fright at his very name:
	this man has tried to obliterate the name of the Nazarene from our people."

---

[18] Acts 9:21.

B 723

مٓن : 115

135	Cultivated, intelligent, and zealous to a fault,[19]
	he will eradicate this deception lest it take hold.
	Renowned and learned, a luminary in the Law,
	his intelligence gives credence to all that he says.
	Highly educated and well versed in Judaism,
140	he knows the scriptures and is a scholar to boot.
	Aflame with zeal and untarnished by falsehood,
	he would, if necessary, give his life for the Law.
	Passionate about the Mosaic Law and steeped in the mysteries of prophecy,
	he would never succumb to falsehood.
145	Conscientiously he went on his way to persecute Jesus.
	No one questions his sincerity or doubts his love of truth.
	The news arrived and incited them (Jews): to give praise.
	Bloodshed was welcomed by approving ears.
	He went on his way carrying menacing letters.[20]
150	He breathed out fury to inflict death upon the disciples.
	When this reckless persecution reached its peak,
	the Persecuted One chose to speak sweetly to him.
	His voice, sounding grieved and perturbed, said to him:
	"Saul, Saul, why do you persecute Me?"[21]

---

[19] Acts 22:3.
[20] Acts 22:5.
[21] Acts 9:4; 22:7.

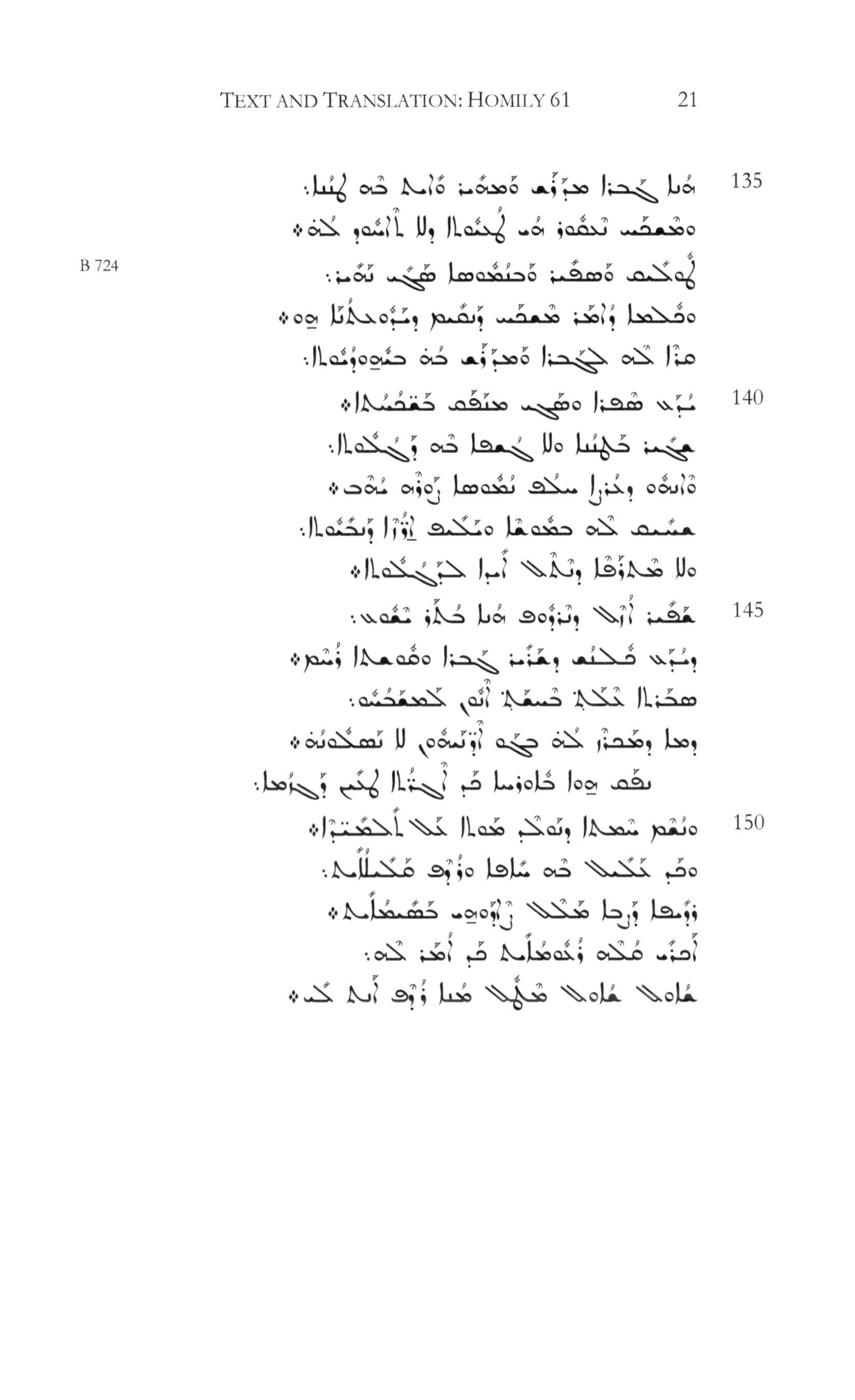

B 724

THE LIGHT THAT SHONE UPON PAUL

155 The voice was disturbed, subdued, full of pain,
but it made Saul listen as though he were the persecuted one before his Persecutor.
As if weary from this weight of persecution,
He was asking him why are you persecuting Me?
He spoke to him with wondrous humility
160 to humble the (huge) pride that was within.
Not with power, not with might, but with great love,
He asked him to clarify his reasons for persecuting Him.
Saul, who had been riding on high, was now left crawling in the dust
for having been persecuted, he confessed and showed forth his humility.
165 "Saul, Saul, why do you persecute Me?
How far and for how long will you (continue) and to what extent will you go?
Give it up! You know how hard it is to kick against the goad.[22]
No more persecution! Abandon this course, it cannot succeed.
If you kick in this crazy way you are bound to take a fall.
170 Come on! Take on the yoke of Crucifixion and be humble.
It is very hard for you to kick against the goad of my Cross.
You will only hurt yourself. Thorns are tough and you are feeble."
He spoke to him with humility and respect
and these won over to wisdom the son of the Hebrews.

---

[22] Acts 9:4; 26:14; 22:7.

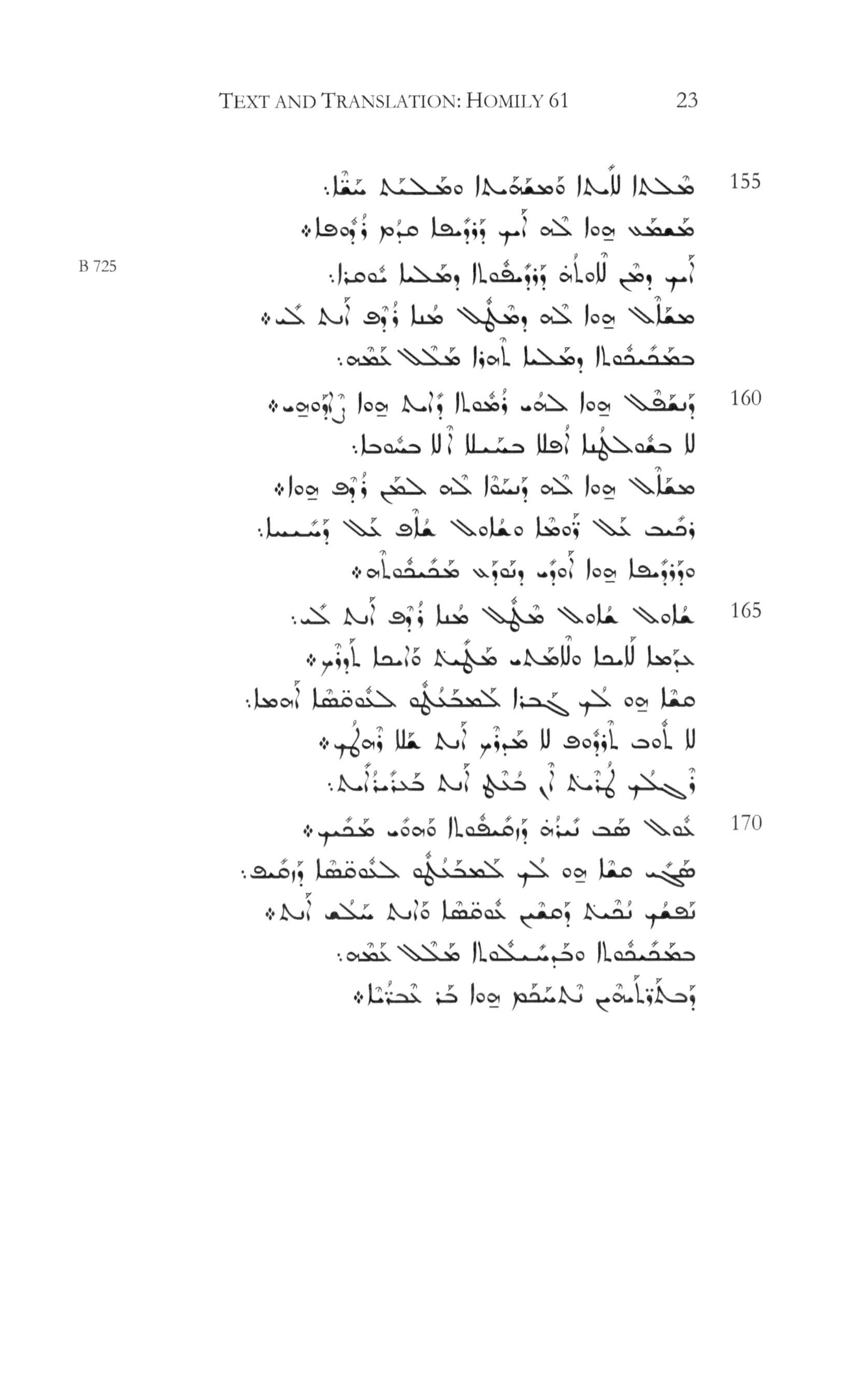

B 725

175 Humbly He was asking, "Why are you persecuting Me?"
Again He advised him, "You should not kick against the goad."
Light poured down upon him and he succumbed to its rays[23]
and by the glory of that light his fire was quenched.
The Word when spoken seeks something other,
180 so that a door will be opened before it and it will be heard.
The key to the door is love—give up all prejudice!
If you accept the key, it will open to you the meaning of everything.
Routine damages the Word and makes it grow cold,
so that if you listen to it by habit it becomes commonplace.
185 But love awakens you to listen with fervour;
if your ear is attuned to the commonplace, it will give you no advantage.
Incline not your ear, but open your heart to this teaching.
It will make you shine more radiantly than the sun.

Light of Gospel

The Gospel is a light, a light that quenches all others.
190 When it shone upon Paul it enlightened him.
At midday, revelation came to the apostle.[24]
Give ear, O prudent one, and lucidly focus your mind.
What kind of light burst forth at midday
to outshine the sun so many times over?

---

[23] Acts 22:11; 9:4–5.
[24] Acts 22:6; 26:13.

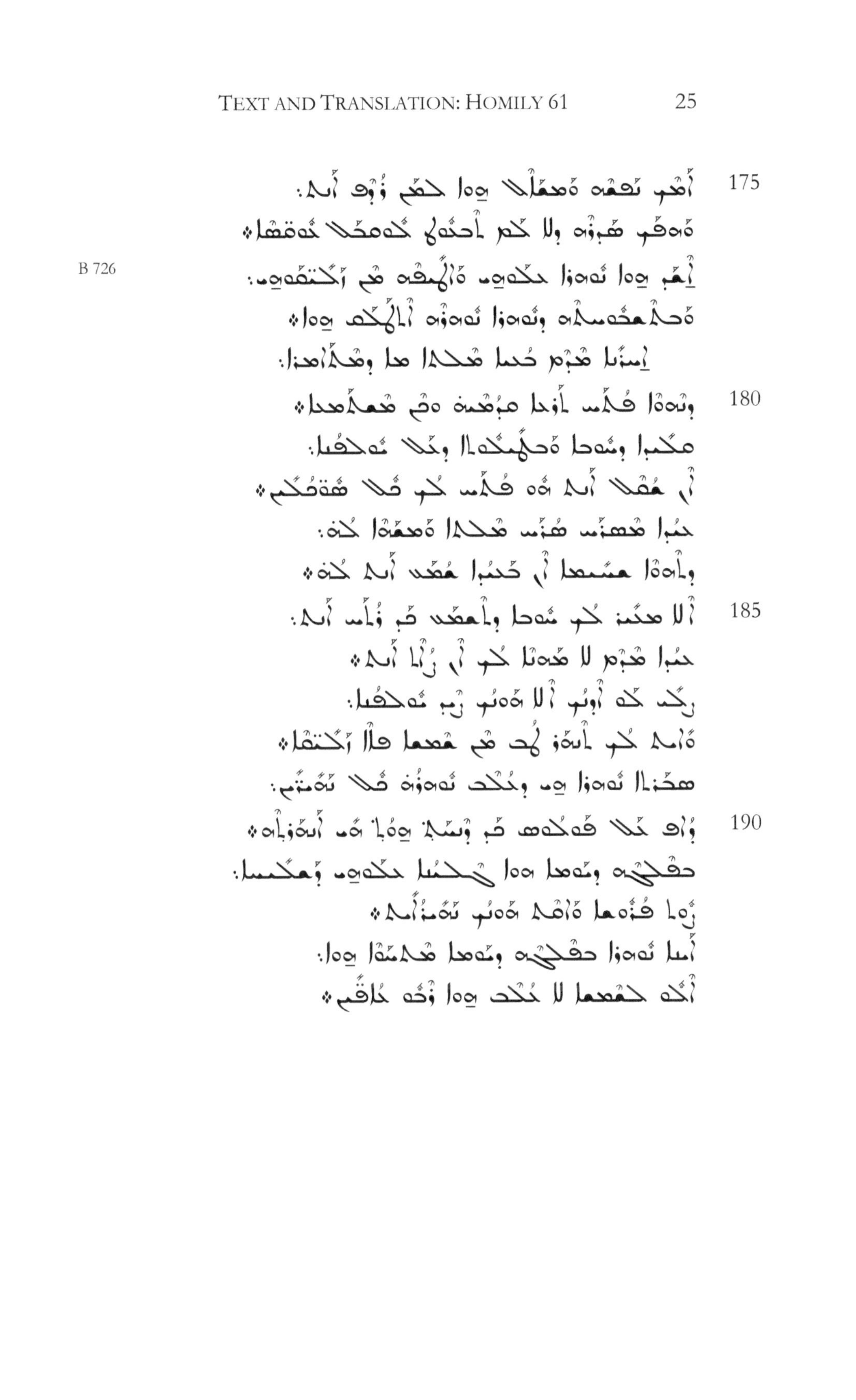

195 In the darkness of night a lamp sheds its ray
but the sun by daytime suppresses all other light.
The Light of the Son shone on Saul at noonday.
It eclipsed the sun with a far greater glory.
When the sun arose to the highest rung of heaven,
200 it blazed from the top of the firmament's arch.
When it had trodden beneath it all the depths of the earth and stood aloft on the highest peak,
all over the world it shed from there its mighty rays to seize the earth.
While it was aflame with the intensity of its great ascent,
an even greater light suddenly rose up and overshadowed it.
205 Had that light not greatly outshone the sun,
it would not have shone forth in the middle of the day nor have been seen by anyone.
It shone in the day, and because of its rays, day became like unto night;
this was to show that in comparison, our sun is no more than a shadow.
In the sea of its brightness, the persecutor's eye was flooded and drowned;
210 he no longer saw any visible things.
His capacity to see retreated into his mind;
his vision turned inside out to reveal hidden beauties within.
Light entered his inner eyes
until it extinguished the light in his outer eyes.

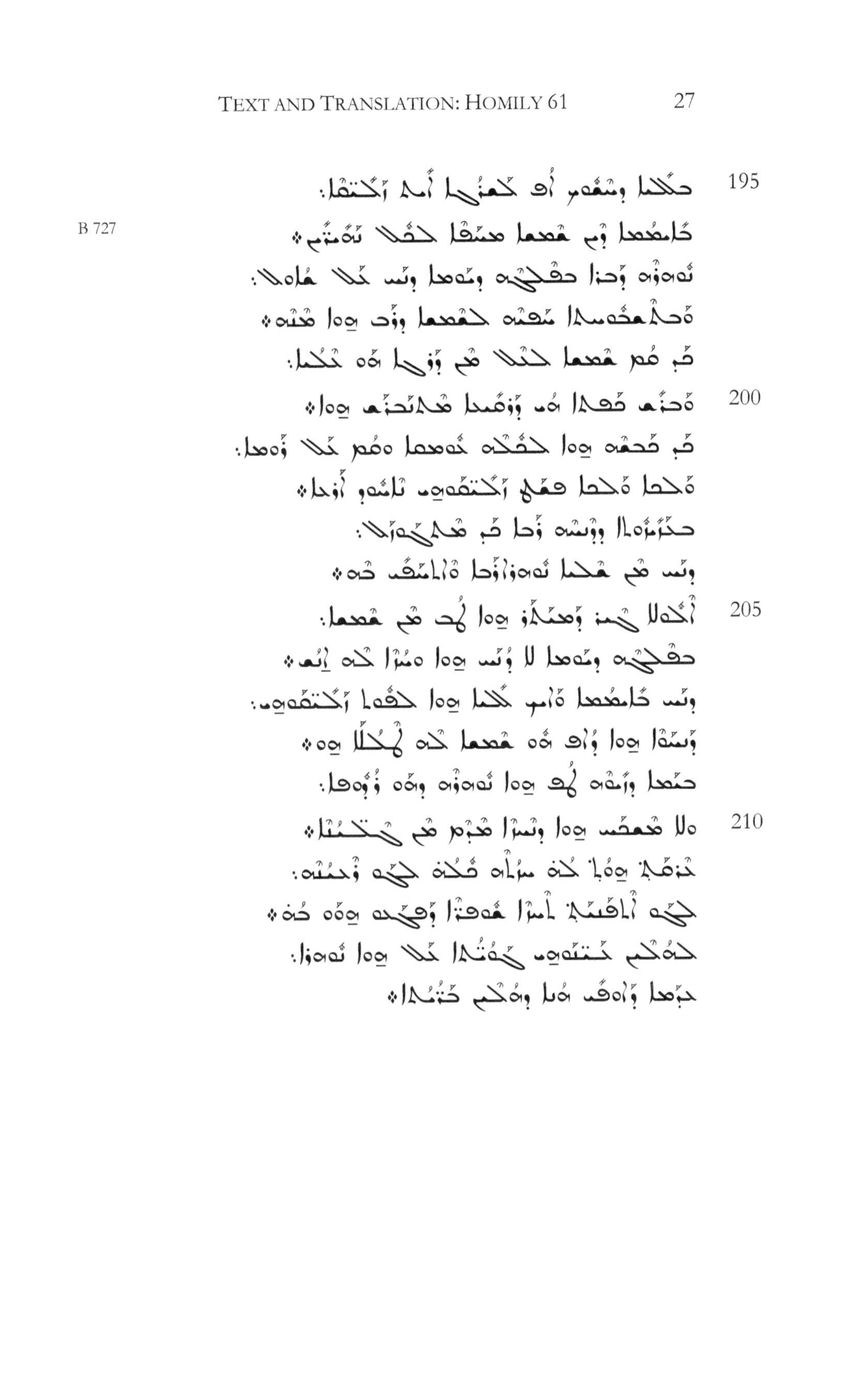

215 "Saul, Saul, why do you persecute Me?"—
He asked him in a powerful but humble voice.
He was lying face downwards, the Light beating on his neck.
That same Light now shining in his inner eye was asking, "Why are you persecuting Me?"
His anger on fire to kill was quenched;
220 his threat focused on the disciples was extinguished.
His letters miscarried and their senders became a reproach;
he annulled the letters and no longer wanted to be called persecutor.
His appearance was that of one persecuted and far from honour,
crestfallen and humiliated because he was asked, "Why do you persecute Me?"

PAUL SPEAKS TO JESUS

225 Then Saul answered Him, "Lord, who are You?"
Once He had entrapped him, he (Saul) became His servant.
"Who are You, Lord?"[25] Saul asked in order to learn more; and our Lord answered him,
"I am Jesus of Nazareth whom you persecute."[26]
The very Name that Saul threatened to eradicate
230 was shown him to be ruler of heaven and all countries (of the earth).
The persecutor had raged against these names:
Neither Jesus nor Nazareth should ever be spoken.
The Son of God vindicated to His persecutor His (apparent) disgrace,
to show him that he would be glorified by that through which salvation comes.

---

[25] Acts 9:5a.
[26] Acts 9:5b.

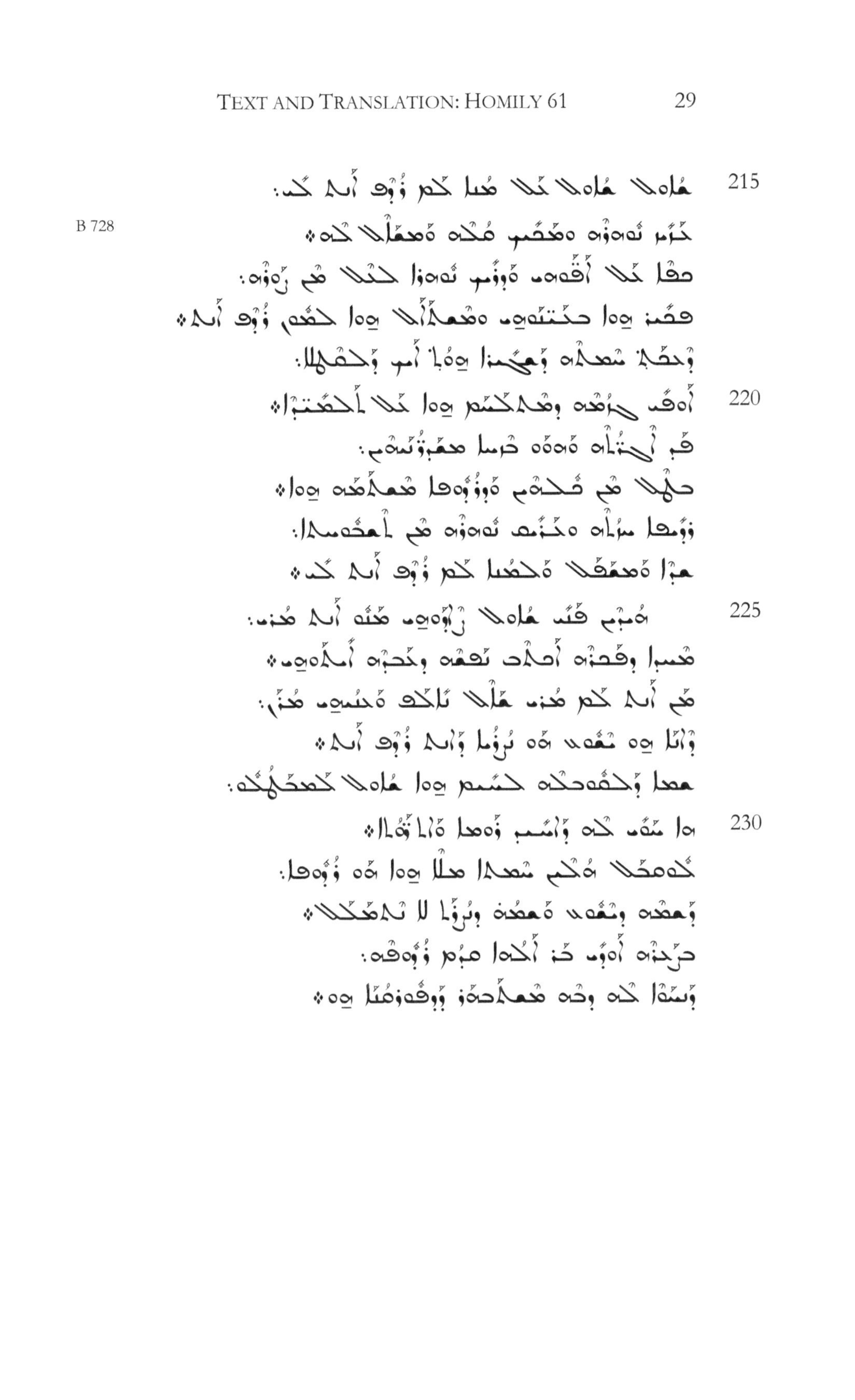

B 728

235   While He was in heaven Nazareth knew no shame;
it was there that the cherished offshoot of his corporeality grew up.
When He desired to come, it was to Nazareth He came
and that is why, while in heaven, He acknowledged her (Nazareth).
I am Jesus, the Nazarene whom you persecute;
240   see if you can dissolve my power as you threaten!
Saul said, "I did not know who You were, O Lord,[27]
but now that I have learnt, I will be as a persecuted one for You.
While I was going astray, I went to persecute the son of Joseph,[28]
not knowing that You are truly the Son of God.
245   I fought against the dead man, who led the Nation astray,
not knowing that You are the Living One who resurrects all.
I looked for You as one that was buried beneath the earth;[29]
I did not reckon that You are exalted above the heights.
I thought You lay powerless in the depths of Sheol;
250   I did not understand that a great Light surrounds You.
I looked for You below (expecting) to see You there in the place of the dead;
no one told me You are fortified with power from the Most High.
I thought You were hidden in (the place of) decay;
I never expected You to address me from on high.

---

[27] Acts 26:15.
[28] Lk. 4:22.
[29] Jn. 19:42; Mt. 27:60; Mk. 15:46.

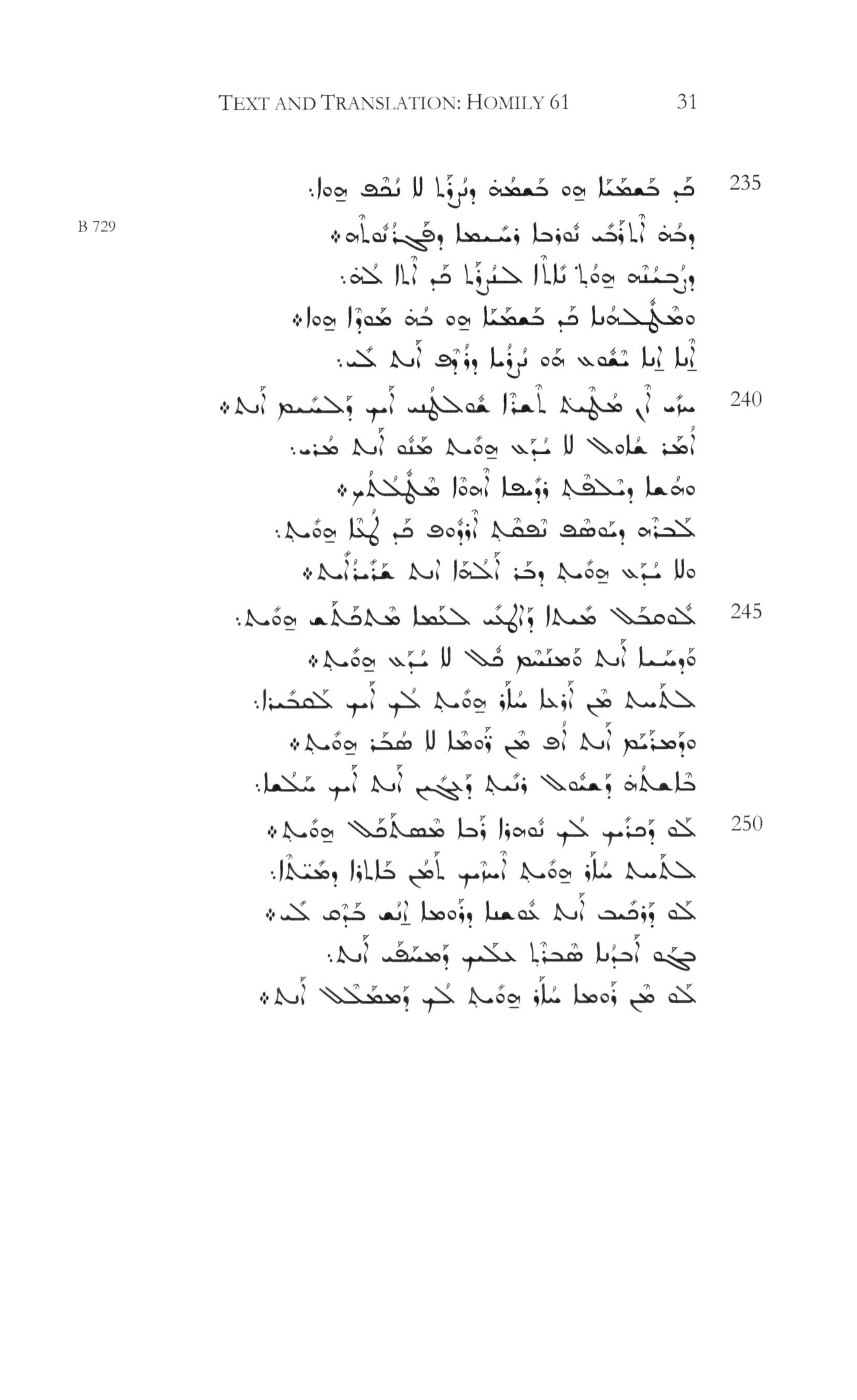

B 729

255   I assumed You were cloaked with a mass of worms;
I did not know that the host of angels praises You.
I thought You were inside the great whirlpool of the dead.
See! Heaven is filled with You but hidden from me.
I thought when I was persecuting, You were sealed within the tomb.
260   I did not know that You are seated at the Father's right hand.
In my mind I assigned You a place beneath the earth;
being blind I did not see that You had descended and (then) ascended.
I was persecuting You because I was obsessed by You.
I expected You to come (to me) but when You did, I did not recognise You.
265   I strove to ensure that no other would come in Your Name,
I attacked and uprooted You so as to disgrace You.
The priests of the Nation misled me and set my face against You,
lest I look at You, see You as You are, and become Yours.
In the Synagogues they showed me that You had broken the Sabbath;
270   they did not tell me that You had fulfilled the whole Law.
I learnt from many that they had hung You on Golgotha;
they did not tell me that Your voice rent the rocks asunder.
One half of Your story they withheld lest I become aware of it;
the other half they embellished to train me as Your oppressor.

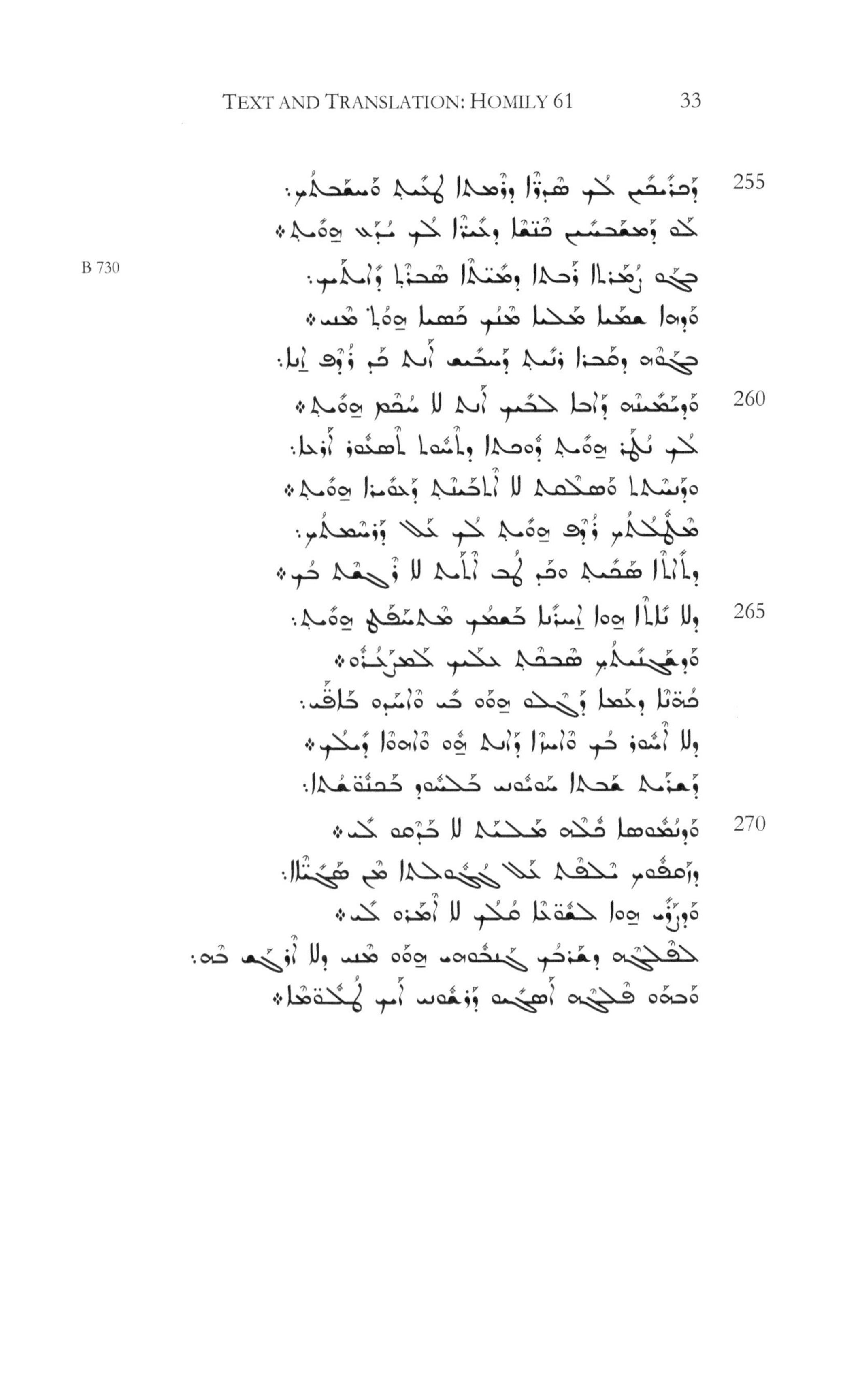

275 I learnt only of the nails they drove into Your hands;
it was hidden from me that You broke the bars of Sheol.
I heard much from them of Joseph's embalming of You;
they did not tell me that at Your resurrection thousands of angels acclaimed (You).
They kept repeating to me that Your descent to Sheol had shut the door in Your face,
280 I never knew that You were exalted above the heights.
I heard from the Jews that the disciples stole You away;
Lord, I did not understand that angels were solicitous over You.
While I was persecuting, I learnt from them that You were the son of a carpenter;
I did not know that You restore all of creation.
285 I thought that You were dead and in the depths of the abyss,
until I saw You on the heights presiding as a judge.
Lo! I regarded you as though a dead one in the abyss of the earth,
I did not know that all of the heights glorify You."
The revelation that Saul received while he was persecuting,
290 was the news that he himself was to be persecuted for Jesus.
Zeal for the house of Adonai went before him with murder and fury.
Light and sound ambushed him on the way that he might never persecute again.
Truly he saw with his eyes and heard with his ears
and then he journeyed onward to preach about the kingdom.

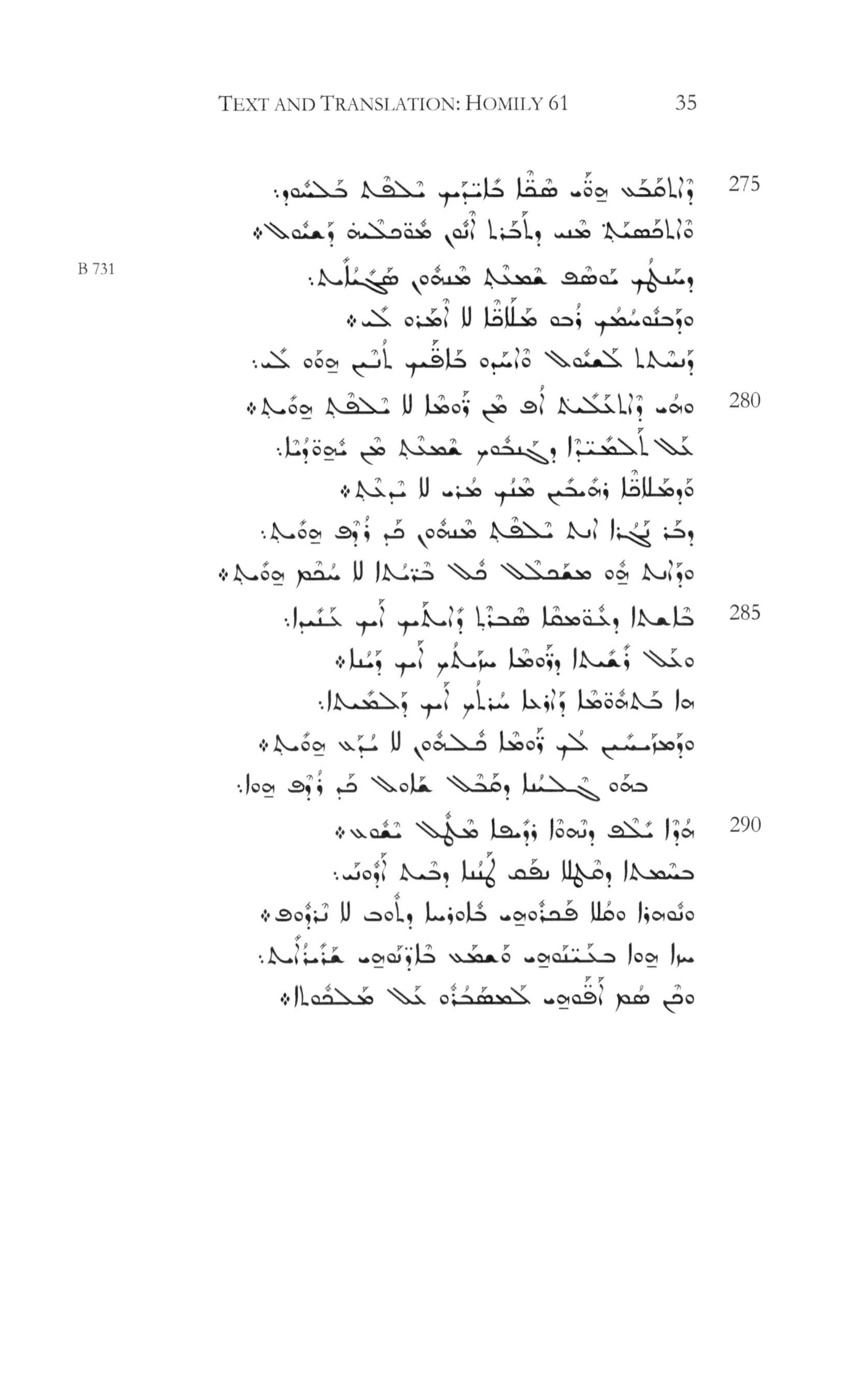

B 731

295	Righteousness saw how fervent was the zeal of that man;
	since he was not rejected, he became worthy of a revelation of the truth.
	The type of man he was, made him fit to be an apostle,
	because he was excellent in things both old and new.
	Being courageous he stood up for the Law to the best of his ability;
300	when revelation called him to the gospel he shone among the apostles.
	While (earthly) time was in shadows, he was a passenger within;
	once the light of Jesus shone through, he was set aflame.
	The Law does not accuse him of any shortcoming.
	The Gospel has no other person comparable to him.
305	He was deeply versed in the mysteries of Moses
	and perceived the beauties of the Crucifixion in everything he saw.
	It was fitting for him to be apostle to the Son;
	because he arranged all those beauties in himself as his own limbs.
	Fasting, vigils and endless toil, as he himself said,
310	was suffering, torment and every kind of distress, for Jesus.
	Every day his endurance in suffering persecution,
	hunger, thirst and poverty, bears witness to me.
	This is the scribe who was converted to the kingdom of Heaven
	because he was conversant with both the old and the new.

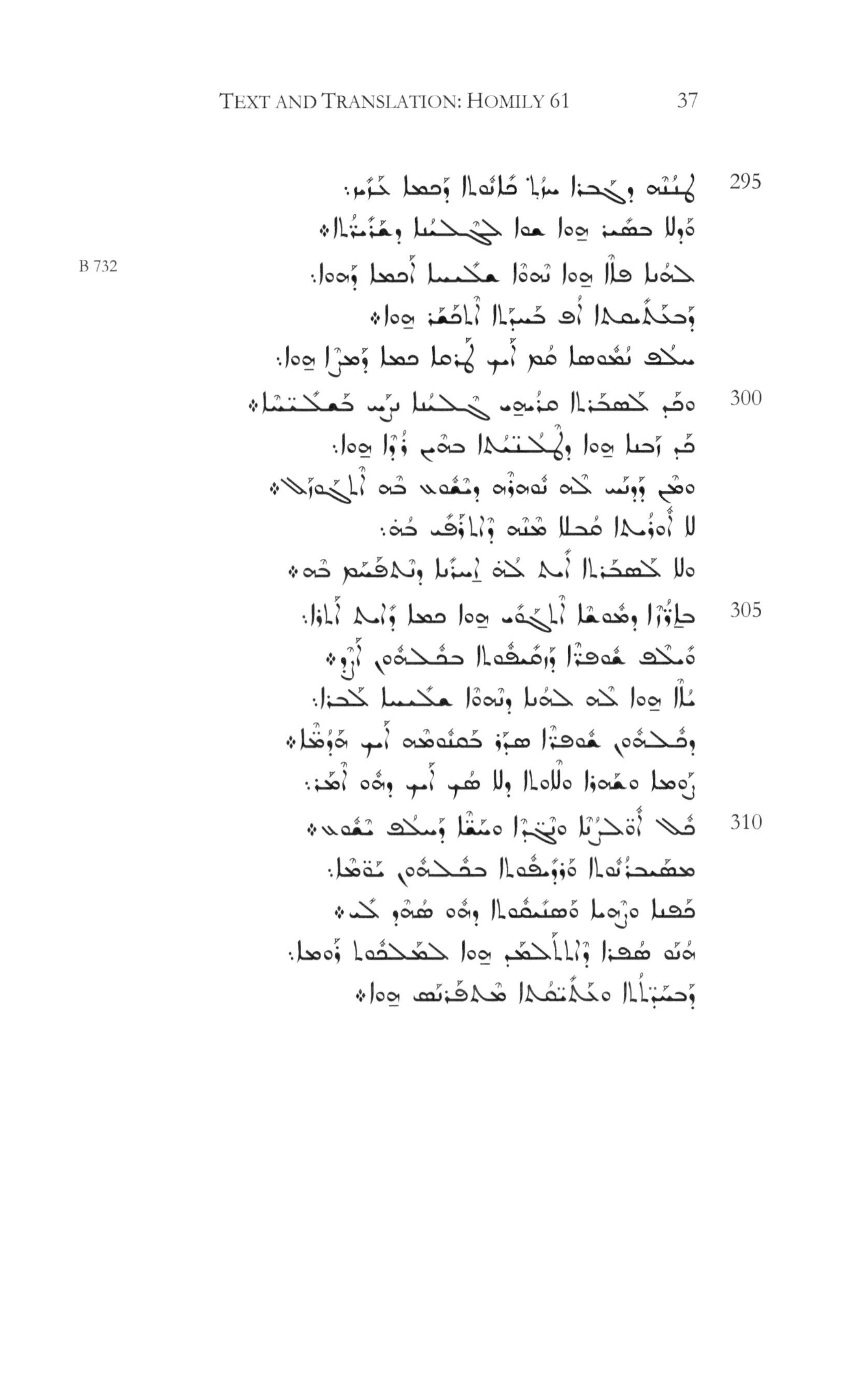

B 732

315   The Gospel enticed him to become its preacher;
      unexpectedly it fell upon him, enlightening him to behold its beauty.
      It saw him—the eloquent, vigilant, zealous, knowledgeable and learned one,
      and seized him to become its advocate among the innocent.
      It shone upon him and, struck by its glory, he fell to the ground;
320   it disclosed to him that it would show all its beauty to him.
      Revelation took him as captive to the third heaven,[30]
      that he might ascend to see the glory of the Son in His high place.
      It cast him down on his face and held his mind captive for the kingdom,
      that he might explain who Jesus was and whose Son He is.

JESUS SPEAKS TO PAUL

325   Saul, Saul, why do you persecute Me?
      It is hard for you to kick against the goad of Crucifixion.
      The persecutor was overwhelmed by the glory that he saw,
      and, as you have heard, could only ask "who are You, Lord?" to the question asked of him.
      He said to him, "I am Jesus of Nazareth,
330   while fighting against the goad, you are persecuting Me.
      Nazareth is small and the dwellers in her few.
      Come! See the heavens and the innumerable assemblies of the Watchful Ones.
      If, as you say, you are threatening a small village,
      what will you do to the great city of the heavenly ones?

---

[30] 2 Cor. 12:2.

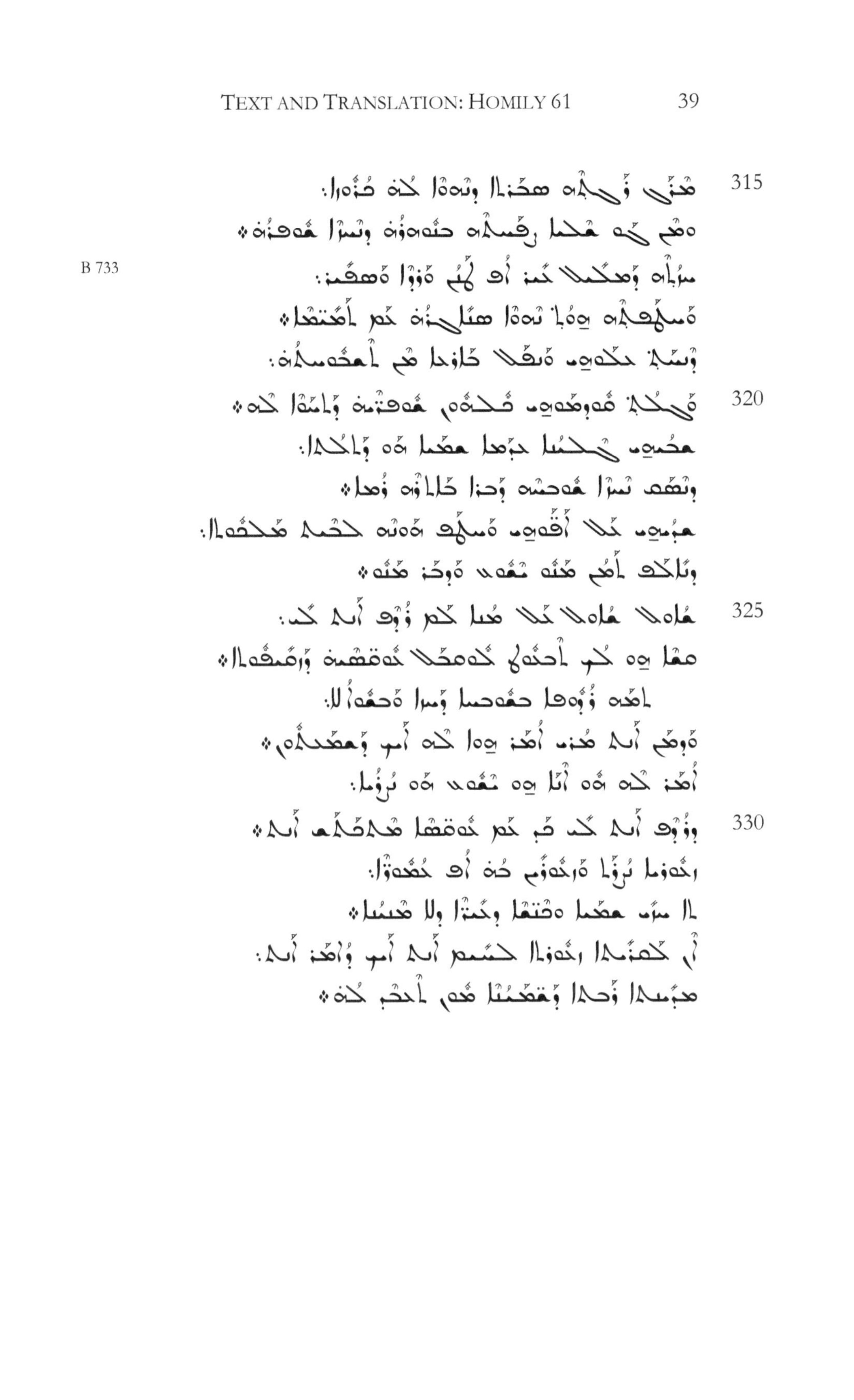

335	If you despise Me for the time I was in Nazareth,
	what will you do to Me who eternally am here?
	If you want to see divine Majesty, come!
	I will show you kingdoms that have no limits to their boundaries.
	If it is a reproach for you to be an apostle of the Nazarene,
340	I am the one from heaven; go, preach Me everywhere!
	I am proud of weakness and am wooed by it,
	even though all the Majesty is Mine, as you can see.
	Now rise and go to the city towards which you were travelling;
	there you will be told what to do."
345	He approached him in a vision and drew him towards Himself.
	As he became wise in hidden things, He called and appointed him.
	The persecutor arose but no sight was in his eyes.
	He opened his eyelids but could see nothing.
	The splendour of the Nazarene blinded his sight,
350	until He authorised his disciple (Ananias) to re-open his eyes.
	It was important that Saul should learn that
	while persecuting these very disciples, Jesus was among them.
	He closed down his vision and bolted the window of his sight;
	He gave to Ananias the key to open it again.

B 734

335

340

345

350

355	He sent him to the disciples who were being persecuted;
	by healing him, his power was subdued by the persecuted ones.
	He rendered blind the famous scribe so that he might know
	his need of the unlearned for the gospel to be illumined.
	He showed him his need for an interpreter,
360	so he might understand the simple power of the Cross.
	Because he was so proud of his own rhetoric,
	his neck was bent before the ignorant that they might cure him.
	Because he thought himself enlightened by his findings,
	he was sent to the disciples to find true light.
365	"Enter into the city and it will be told you what to do":[31]
	why this, if not to shame him before the disciples?
	Saul began to travel on the way and they lead him,
	the newly blinded one, that he might enlighten the world by his proclamation.
	His soul was filled with great light from the revelation
370	when, by a stratagem, outer light was removed from his eyes.
	Because he went out to persecute the Light, He (the Light) made him blind
	so that he might return a witness to the Light once he was enlightened.
	He entered the city, as we said, and they were drawing him.
	The priests welcomed him because they heard he was zealous.

---

[31] Acts 9:6.

B 735

 (sic) .

375	They rejoiced over him because he had come to inflict sufferings on the followers of Jesus;
	they welcomed him as a hero and rejoiced over him.

THE DIALOGUE BETWEEN JEWISH PRIESTS AND PAUL

	The priests of the Nation were saying these things to him:
	"For a long time we have been waiting for one of your thoroughness.
	Sir, we have heard of the zeal in which you were clad
380	against Jesus who deceived both our people and his disciples.
	We learned of the sufferings you made them endure,
	men and women who confess His Name, and we praise you greatly.
	Reports were reaching us about the ardour of your zeal:
	the multitudes you have arraigned for confessing His Name.
385	They told us of the anger with which your mind was consumed
	against this heretic and the foolish people he deceived.
	Today we will witness your vehemence about which we have heard.
	Arise as an expert and with you we will bind them.
	Show us here the mightiness of your zeal,
390	we have been looking forward to seeing you so that you will help us.
	Those who were led astray after Jesus troubled the earth
	will be weeded out from among us by your diligent help."
	Saul says, "Now, I'll have my say!
	Don't be quick to take action; because it is not our concern.

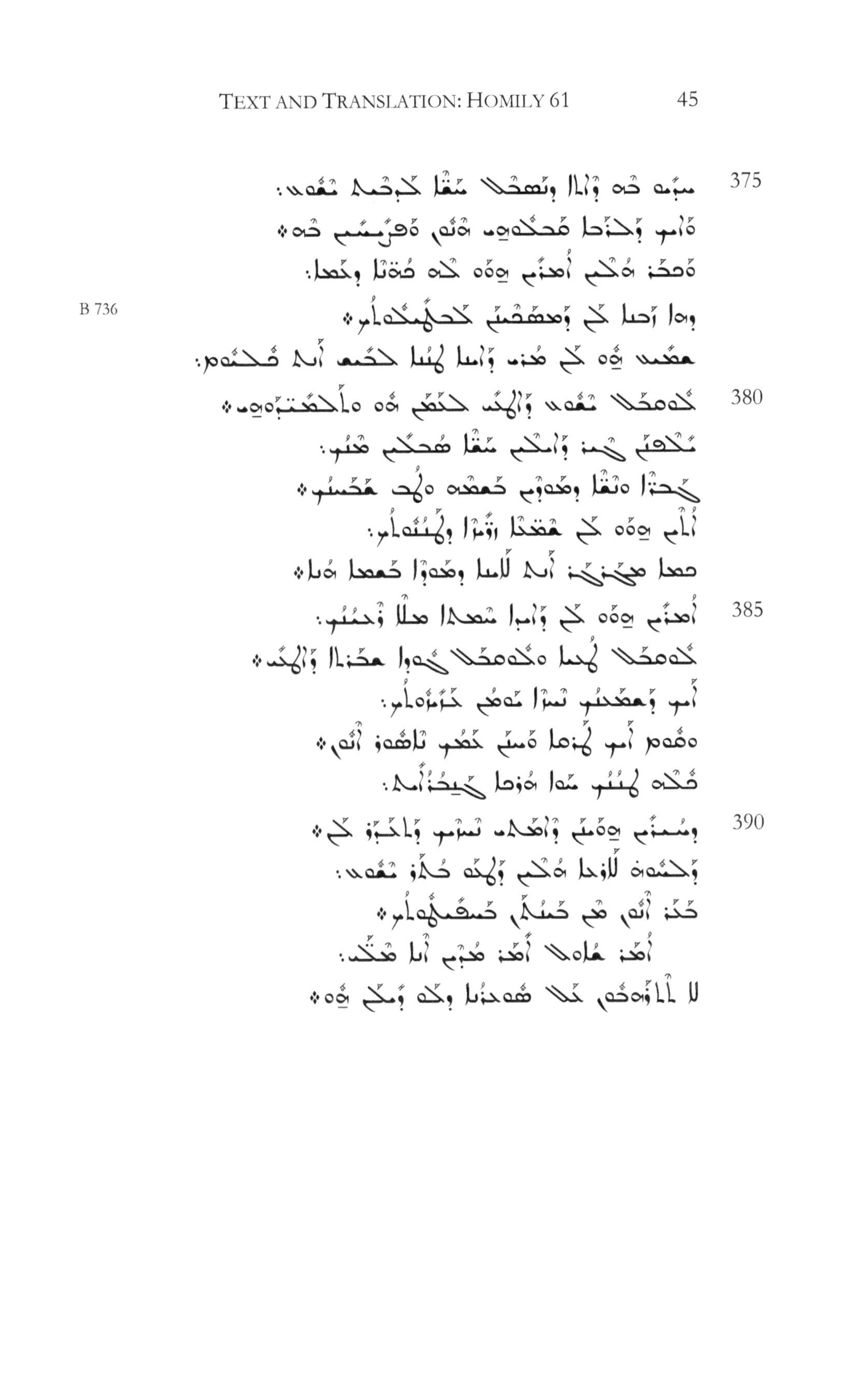

B 736

395	The son of the carpenter took the light from my eyes as a pledge.
	Go and bring me the pledge taken from me which I will accept.
	He closed the doors of my eyes while I was coming on the road.
	I will love Him who can now reopen them.
	Henceforth do not judge me on what you have heard,
400	because there is something new I have to say and proclaim to you.
	keep this sign (of my blindness) until I can see (again).
	As I have said: Who will give me the light of my eyes?
	Let Scribes, Pharisees, and Sadducees come!
	Can any of them by their power restore light to my eyes?
405	This is an open trial and it is as plain as day;
	I am right in the middle; I will indicate whoever opens my eyes.
	This is my longing: to see who has the light?
	I will trust the one who can actually open my eyes.
	I am in darkness, I seek the one who can give me light;
410	I will listen and not dispute anything he has to say to me."
	The priests say, "What is this you are saying?
	If what you say is true, are you devising a way of testing us?
	Perhaps, being clever, you are speaking deceitfully;
	Anyone here who acknowledges Jesus will have to endure suffering.

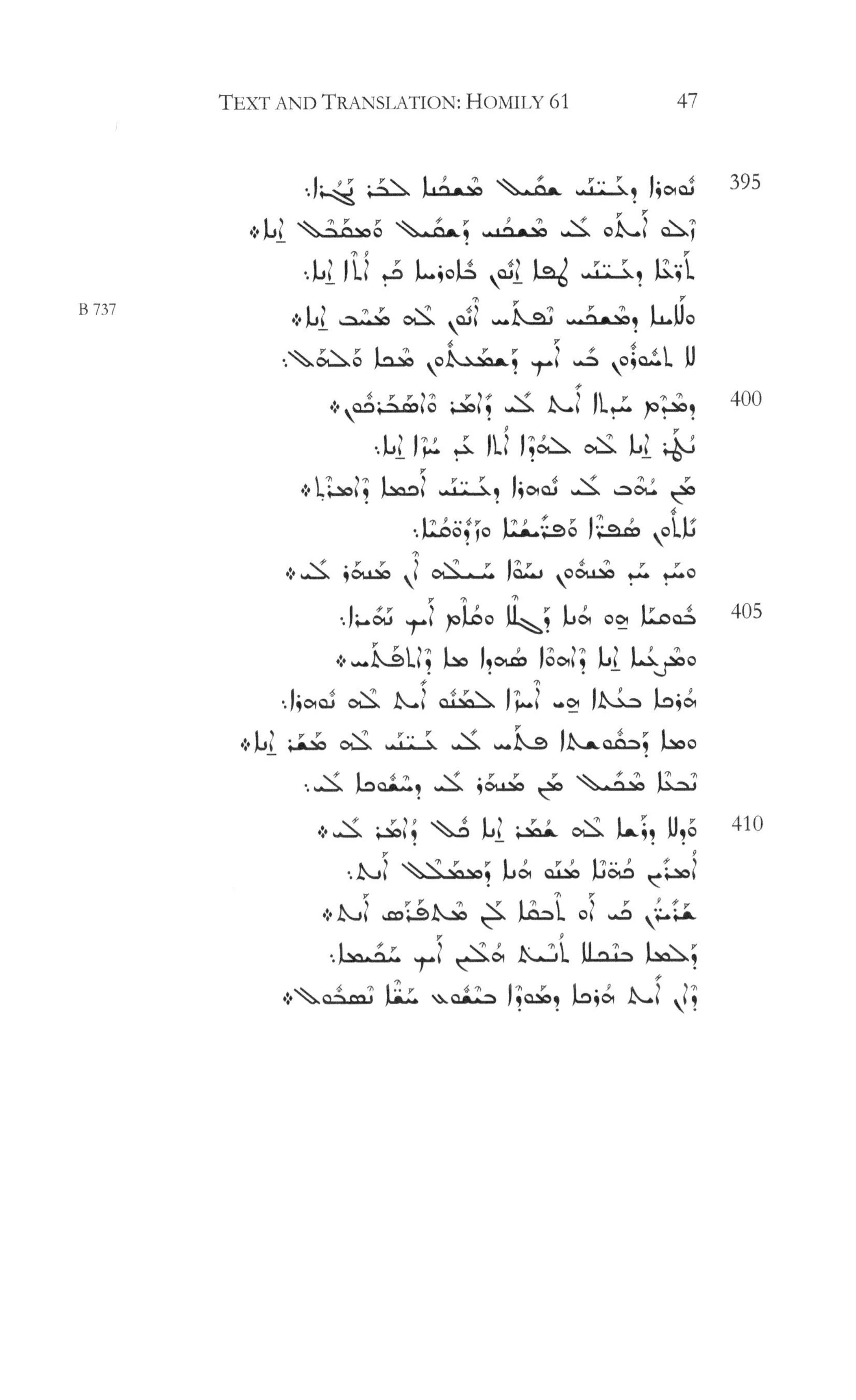

B 737

415 Unswervingly we placed our trust in your fidelity.
Hand over the letters since we have heard why you have come."
Saul says, "I do not speak deceitfully;
I preach the truth I have learned and the things I have seen.
When I received the letters to take (with me), I was my old self
420 but on the way Christ met me and made me new.
Look! I am tearing up the letters as you can see,
so that you can believe my word that I do not approve of my former deeds.
The building I then built, I (presently) pull down.
From now on I will build on the foundation of Jesus Christ.
425 Unlike you I saw Jesus, whom you treat with contempt,
(robed) in a glory that earthly beings cannot explain.
I am ripping up the letters while I am still blind,
for I cannot bear to see Him shamed in these writings.
Having beheld his glory I can no longer dishonour Him.
430 I am intoxicated by His love from which I can no longer depart.
With God Saul exchanged light for light;
in place of his previous enlightenment he received another even greater.
The sun of righteousness shone in his mind
and its rays extinguished all the light that was outside.

TEXT AND TRANSLATION: HOMILY 61   49

B 738

Dialogue between Jesus and Ananias

435 By his wisdom the son of the carpenter outwitted the lion,
He summoned Ananias, his disciple, to come and see him[32].
He established His truth by the things He did;
sending a persecuted one to restore light to the persecutor.
The disciples were fleeing from Saul[33]
440 because he was persecuting them wilfully and without mercy.
They heard a report that he was in a rage and on his way to kill.
Out of fear of him they went into hiding.
Shaken and afraid they hid themselves away.
(Until) the Lord told Ananias in a vision to go to him.
445 "Stand up, come, go and see Saul and lend him a hand.
I have shown you to him; even before you go he will believe in you."
In the vision he has seen, I told him your name and what you are like.
He is expecting you. Do not delay his work (that Paul has to do).
Ananias heard the account of Saul and was terrified.
450 He began to beg that he might not have to go to the persecutor.
"Lord, since when did he become so close to your disciples?
Is this not a ruse to further injure and destroy?
When did the wolf learn to feed with the lambs and love them?
Who can feed the hawk alongside the fledglings?

---

[32] Acts 9:10–16.
[33] Acts 9:26.

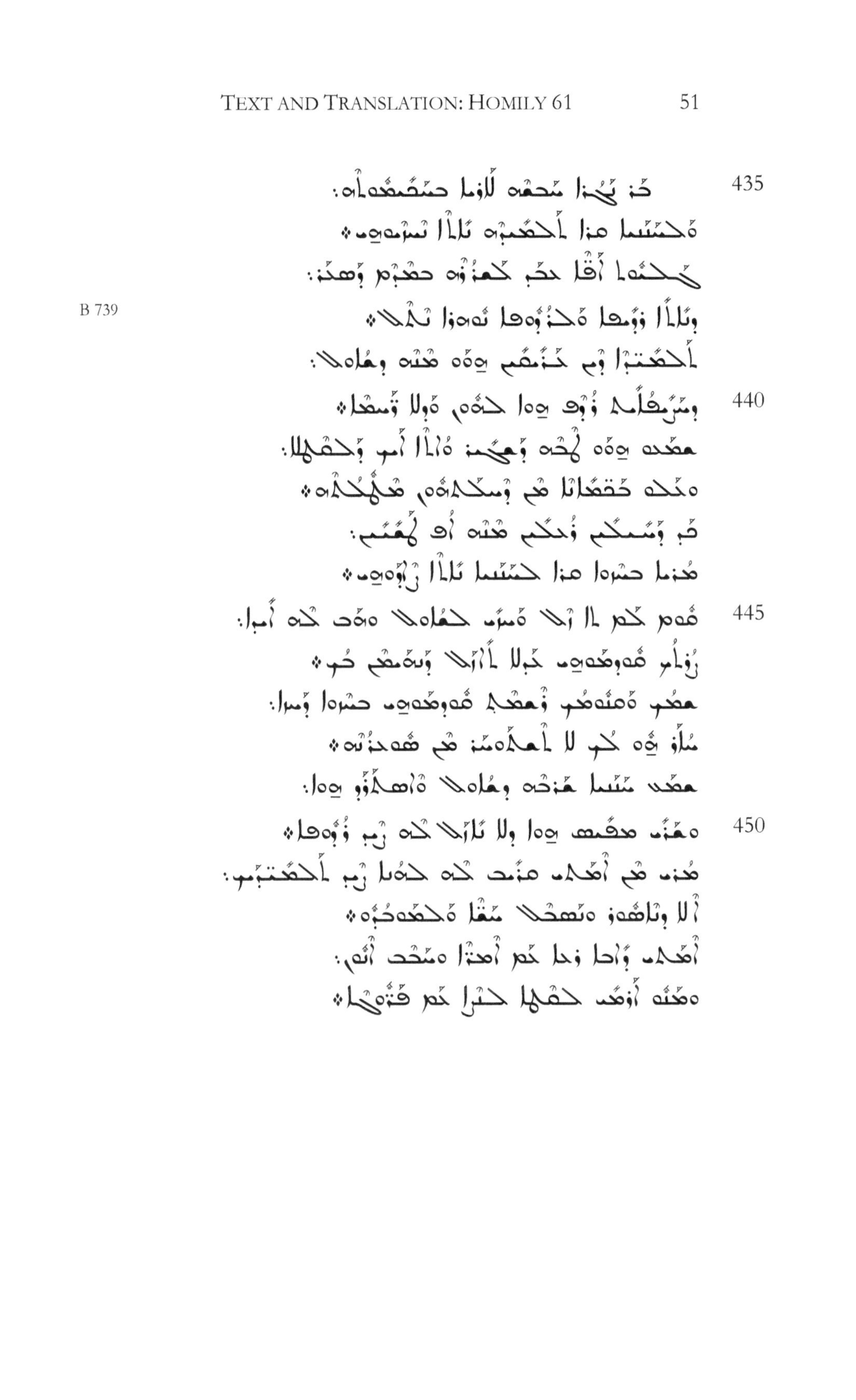

455	Who can put a snake in the nest of a dove?
	How can this man possibly join with your disciples?"
	"Go Ananias", said our Lord, "take courage;
	Look! The lion has been captured, his strength reduced, and he is waiting for you.
	I have bound the wolf and it now stays with the lambs tame and serene;
460	the cruel one has been subjugated and will not harm you.
	Behold the mighty one is bound in darkness and his strength has been broken;
	go and free him because he is exhausted and weary.
	Come and see! Behold the lion eats straw like a bull
	and is pressed down like you under the yoke of crucifixion.
465	Go, see the skilful scribe who has ended his words.
	And look! He has wrapped himself in simplicity from now on.
	He is my chosen vessel in whom the gospel will be poured;
	he will comprehend it as his heart has been enlarged."
	I will endeavour to praise Paul though I cannot achieve it;
470	the foot of this homily is higher than my head. How can I speak of him?
	What ordinary person can depict such a king,
	not knowing to distinguish colours and pigments?
	Who is capable of producing an admirable portrait of Paul,
	except the finger of the godhead by which he is adorned.

455
460
465
470

475 Afterwards He openly called him His chosen vessel.
Who can improve the beauty of a beautiful one?
With discernment He wisely selected his chosen one;
His goodness caused the chosen one to devote himself to Him.
His election is something prized for he put on beauty at his renewal.
480 He who is upright chose him; he who was chosen grasped it with his freewill.
"This chosen one is my vessel and a very fitting one for me;
he will carry my name among the gentiles and among kings[34].
He has much to suffer on my account[35] when he preaches about me.

THE ENCOUNTER BETWEEN PAUL AND ANANIAS

Go therefore Ananias, open his eyes.
485 By the mouth of the Lord the chosen one who became famous is extolled;
How could I suppose to have worthily extolled his beauty?
The disciple obeyed the word of the Lord as he was commanded;
he went and gave light to the blind eyes of Saul.
He came towards him and put his hand over his eyes.
490 A light appeared inside his darkened pupils.[36]
He called Saul, "my brother", to show him that he is his brother;
Paul will also acknowledge the family into which he was admitted.
"Our Lord Jesus who met you has sent me to you
and by my hands has sent you light from His treasury."[37]

---

[34] Acts 9:15.
[35] Acts 9:16.
[36] Acts 9:18.
[37] Acts 9:17.

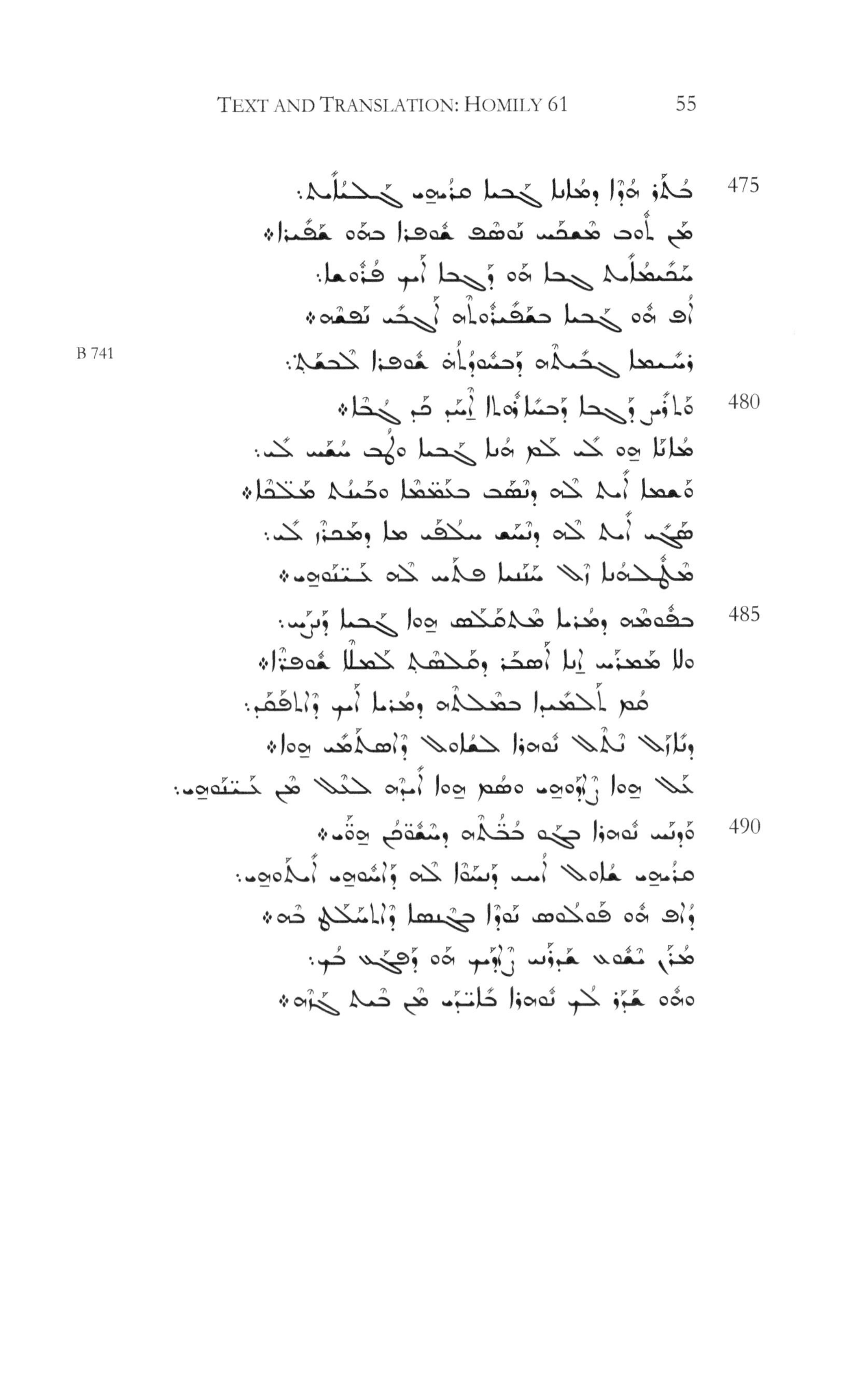

B 741

495 Paul said, "Yes, you are truly from Him,
because everyone who has light radiates it on all sides.
The light was cupped in your hand, O fellow man, as it approached me;
streams of brightness poured from your fingers.
You are a disciple of Him whom I saw, since streams of brightness (also) surrounded Him,
500 waves of light in whose rays the eyes are bathed.
You are from Him in whose light I saw glory,
some tiny portion from that infinite sea."
Saul, the scribe, was questioned by Ananias.
By the disciple's efforts the skilled orator put on Christ.
505 He opened to him the door of baptism and confirmed him
in the new womb that each day begets beautiful things.
He purified the chosen vessel in the divine water,
So the gospel might fall on one capable of receiving it.
From inside the womb of baptism, Paul emerged with eagerness.
510 His voice is powerful and better than that of his fellow apostles.
Who like him has looked at the cross and received from it
the new light of all the beauty it proclaims.

JESUS IS SOLE ROLE MODEL OF JESUS

Who looks like him? For he looks completely like Christ.
"You should imitate me as I am in Christ."[38]

---

[38] 1 Cor 11:1.

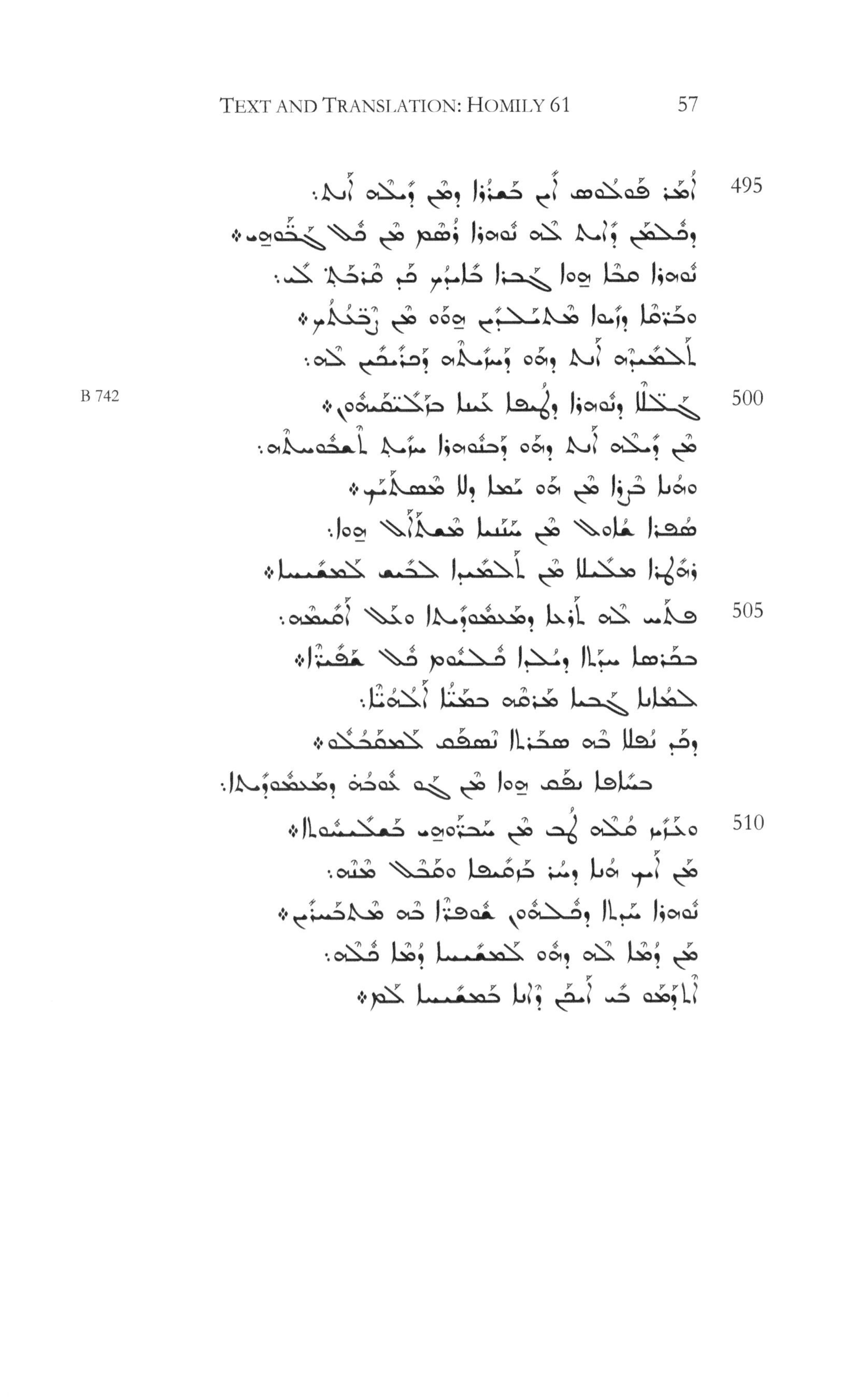

515	The word is so great that the very hearing of it makes human nature surpass itself.
	The intellect was stunned and the mind conquered from hearing this very word.
	Paul looked neither at the first word nor at the last word,
	he looked to the heights, to the beauty of Christ so that he might imitate Him.
	Although there were ten thousand varieties of beautiful people,
520	he outshone them all; nor could he imitate anybody but Jesus.
	When Melchizedek[39] was placed before him as a mirror,
	he did not look at him; his vision clung to Christ.
	He did not imitate the glorious Enoch[40] who did not taste death;
	he earnestly desired to imitate his Lord who was killed.
525	He was not content to keep a fast like Elijah's,[41]
	his fast was in the footsteps of Christ.
	He did not look to imitate the wonders of Moses.[42]
	He desired to attain the image of the sufferings of Christ.
	All those beauties are commonplace in comparison to that beauty;
530	he does not wish to imitate anyone but his Lord.
	When he ascended he rose above the images of all the just,
	he immersed himself in Christ and not in any other.
	He set aside the virtue of all the upright;
	he did not intend to imitate it, but only Jesus.

---

[39] Gen 4:18; Ps 110:4; Heb 5:6, 10; 6:20; 7:10, 11, 15, 17.
[40] Heb 11:5.
[41] 1 Kings 19:8.
[42] Ex 11:10.

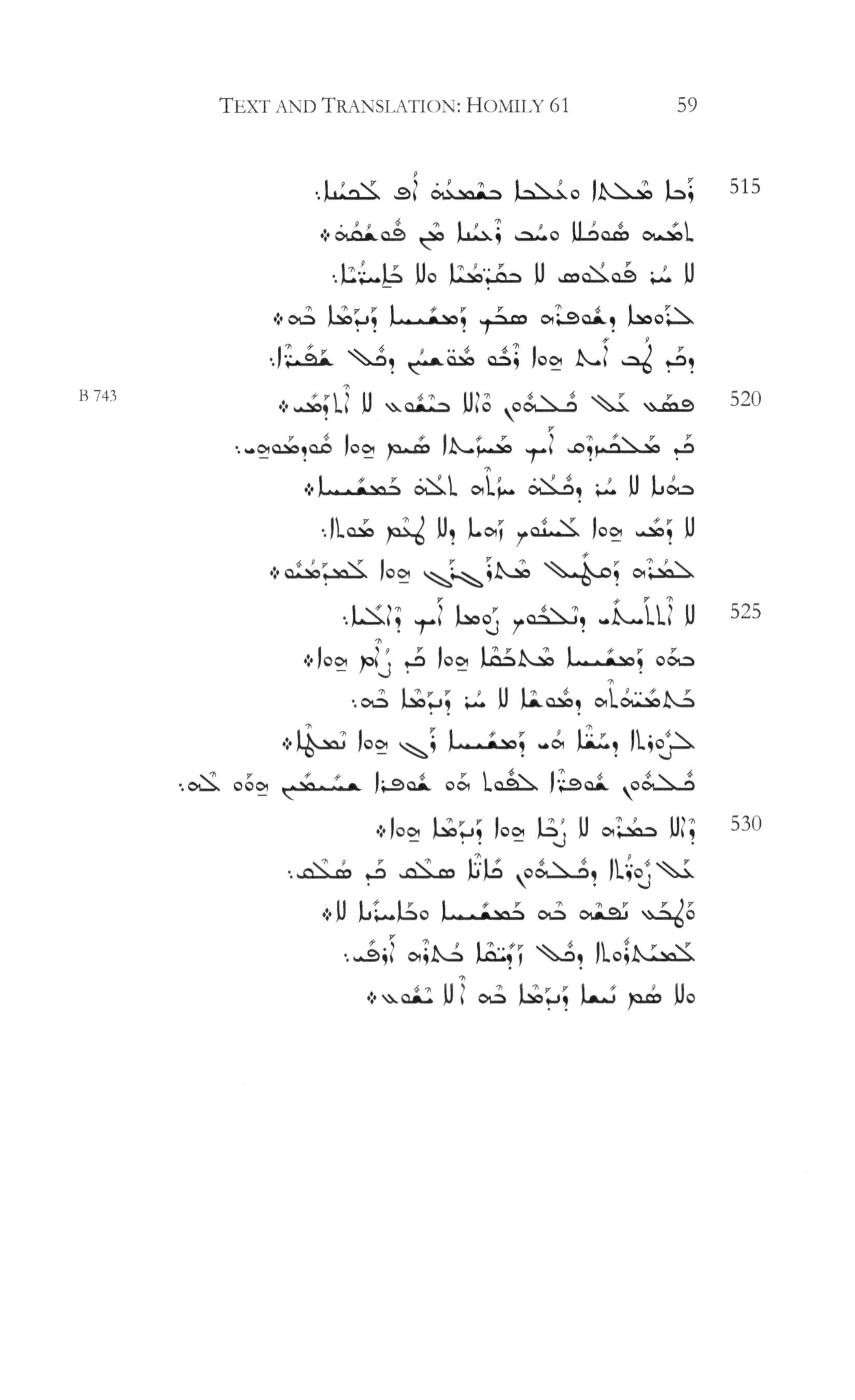

535	"Imitate me as I imitate Christ."[43]
	Great is the example he set himself and imitated.
	What need to say anything further about beauty?
	There is no homily to depict his beauty which is manifold.
	Who can describe his image in words that do not misrepresent?
540	He resembles his Lord whose image as Son is transcendent.
	He is alive and yet, as he said, is not living.
	"For it is Christ alone who lives in me,"[44] he only confessed.
	This is a wonder beyond all that we have ever wondered;
	the capacity of our ears cannot contain the magnitude of it.
545	He resembles completely all that is above, while remaining below;
	he is not in any way like Him, yet lives in Him and speaks.
	"Christ lives in me, it is not I who is living,[45] he says.
	"I died in Him who truly died for me."
	"The old man in us was crucified with Him;"[46]
550	all lustful impulse expired on the cross.
	Who is the one who did not live for Himself while alive?
	But when He died, He died for him.
	Who can mortify his instincts and his thoughts,
	if his perception has not been swapped for the perception of Jesus?

---

[43] 1 Cor 11:1.
[44] Gal 2:20.
[45] Gal 2:20.
[46] Rom 6:6.

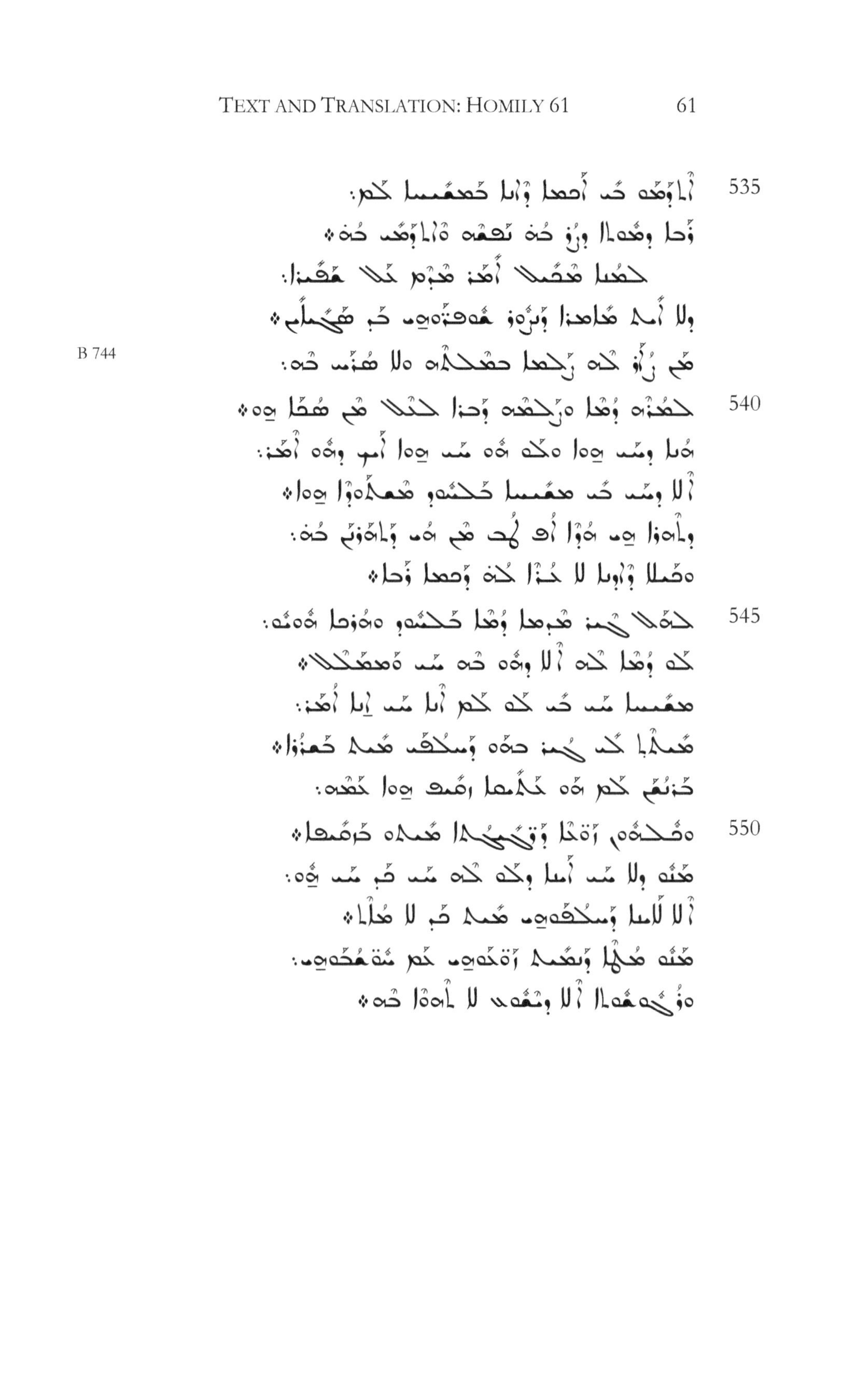

555   How did Paul arrive at this situation?
He could imitate the perfection of his Friend.
Who is able to step outside himself as he had done?
"Love drew me out and replaced me with Christ."
O human one, what are you saying about your Apostleship?
560   Your words can't be understood by mortal ears unless you moderate them!
Who can possibly go out from you except your own self?
Or who else but yourself can enter and dwell within you?
"Love has removed me and brought Christ to dwell within me."
The indweller is great and He who possesses him is great and excellent.
565   He was not perturbed nor was he aware of anyone but Jesus;
He lived in Him and he was doing His will.

CROSS AND PAUL

He looked resolutely at the cross
and all carnal impulses were extinguished within him.
He looked at the cross and could see all of its beauty
570   and therefore he boasts of it alone.
"I will not boast of anything except in it."[47]
He became aware of its riches and so he boasted of it.
He understands it as the cause of all good things;
he possesses nothing as great as it.

---

[47] Gal 6:14.

TEXT AND TRANSLATION: HOMILY 61

B 745

575 He looked at the sign of shame and saw in it a myriad of virtues.
And this became a (source of) pride each day as he preached.
That revelation made him go forth to many countries,
but he found no beauty in any of them to match the cross.
He penetrated deeply all the treasures of theology
580 and did not find anything to match the beauty of the cross.
He studied to perfection all that perfection might imply
and stopped here because in the crucifixion everything is made perfect.
And because he found all beauty perfected there,
he preached nothing but the cross wherever he went.
585 He crucified himself to his love of the cross;
and he crucified the world to the cross as well.
He said, "The world is crucified to me and I to the world."[48]
What marvellous power to be able to crucify the whole world!
What kind of man could carry the whole world hung on the cross?
590 He alone could carry (so heavy) a burden.
What strong man can lift this stone aloft but Paul
who crucified himself to the world, as he said?
He crucified himself to the world and the world to him;
by the power of the crucifixion he hoisted up himself and the world.

---

[48] Gal. 6:14.

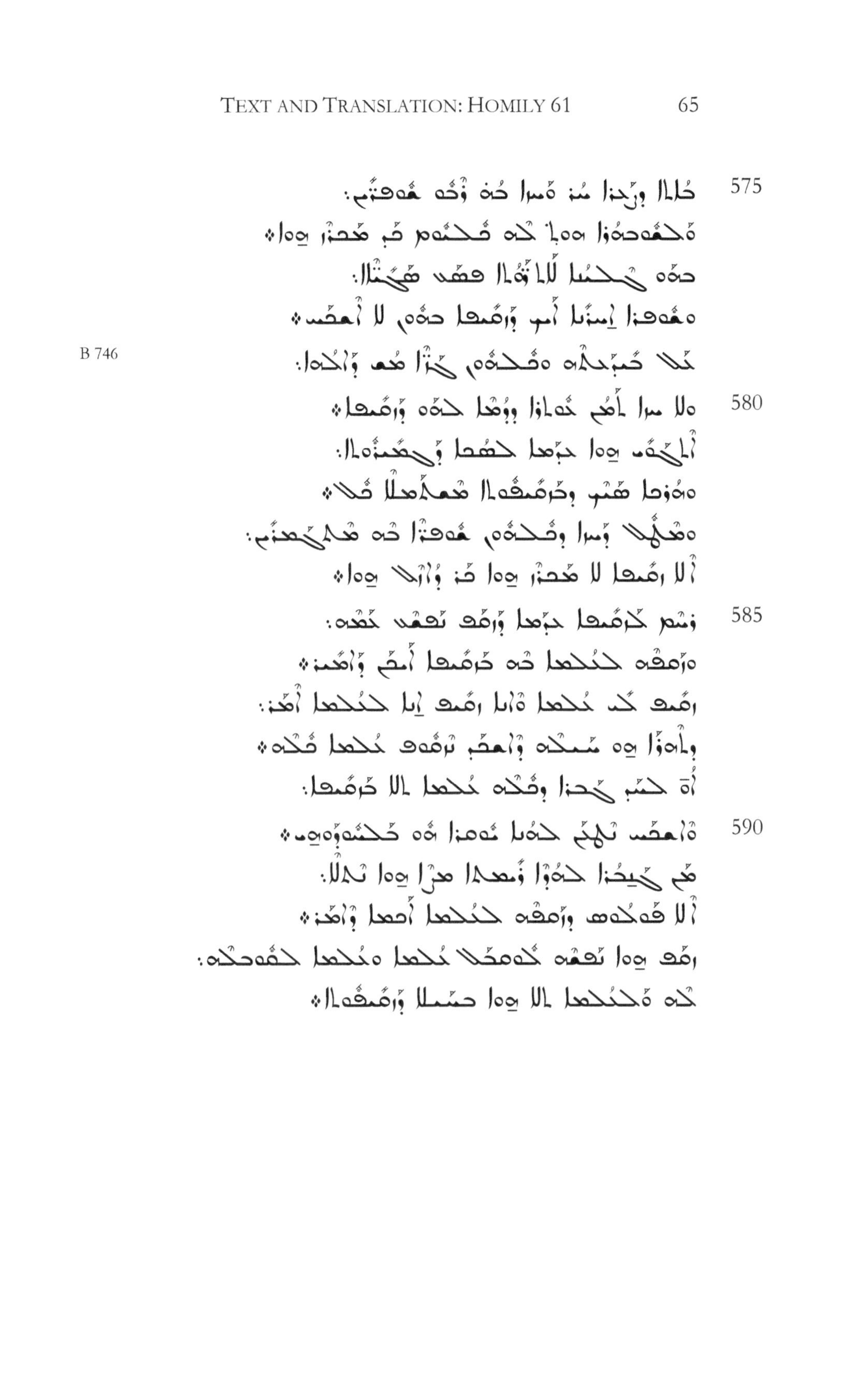

595 "I am crucified to the world,"[49] he said, "For it is no longer I who live."[50]
These words mean that he died to the world and is alive in God.
How do I dare to praise this man?
What words of mine could contain the sea of his discourse?
In my wonderment I will now desist from praising him;
600 blessed is He who chose him for apostleship, for he is worthy of it.

---

[49] Gal 6:14.
[50] Gal 2:20.

595 ܪܡܝܟ ܐܢܐ ܠܚܘܫܒܐ ܗܘ ܗܘ ܘܐܡܪ ܘܠܐ ܟܠܡ ܡܢ ܐܢܐ܆
ܗܫܐ ܘܡܢܟܕܘܝܢ ܗܟܝܠ ܗܘܐ ܠܚܘܫܒܐ ܕܡܢ ܠܐܠܗܐ܀
ܠܗܢܐ ܓܝܪ ܐܝܬ ܐܘܗܝ ܠܡܗܦܟܘܬܗ܂
ܘܠܐ ܗܟܝܠ ܐܢܐ ܚܢܢܐ ܘܗܪܟܘܗܝ ܠܡܗܦܢܘܬܗ܀
ܐܠܐ ܡܢܝ ܗܝ ܦܘܠܚܢܗܘܗܝ ܕܝ ܐܝܘܢ ܐܢܐ܆

B 747

600 ܕܐܢܝ ܗܘ ܕܓܒܝܘܗܝ ܠܡܟܫܢܐܠ ܘܗܢܐ ܗܘܐ ܟܢܗ܂
ܥܠܝܗܝ܂

Homily 62: A Second Homily on Paul the Apostle

Reason for writing a second mimro on St Paul the Apostle

I have not recounted the story of Paul as befits him,
nor when I was speaking about him, did I really say anything at all.
Yes, I spoke, but I fell silent and said no more.
For this reason I want to speak, for my treatment of him was inadequate.

5   What I left unsaid, you will now learn
for I am ready to tell of him, if only I can.
What I did not express, I am eager to speak about now;
you have not yet heard a thing, so listen now to what I say.
His story is even greater than the sea and its floods

10   for he conquered the sea when he descended into it, as he related.[1]
Shipwrecked he survived in the sea night and day;[2]
the strong waves were howling yet he was not overcome.
The winds of the sea were dashing against him and he endured,
because he disregarded weariness, dishonor and every misfortune.

15   Daily he gloried in all his infirmities[3]
and he considered his weakness to be his strength.
He declared, "When I am weak, then I am strong."[4]
He showed that he placed no confidence in his bodily limbs.
With a sound soul but a sickly body

---

[1] 2 Cor. 11:25–26.
[2] 2 Cor. 11:25.
[3] 2 Cor. 11:21–30.
[4] 2 Cor. 12:10.

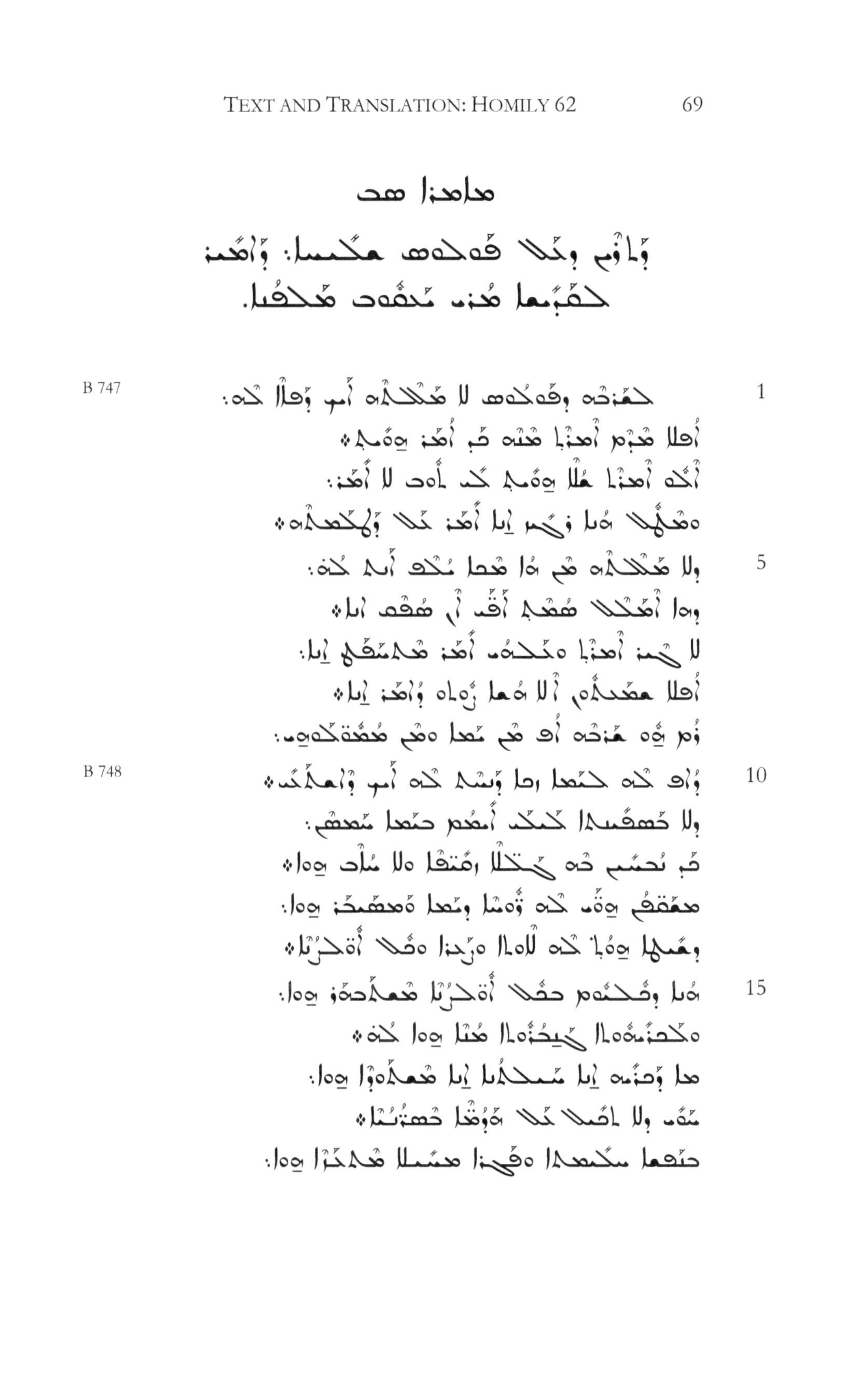

20	he endured the sufferings he faced and did not waver.
	Despite his frailty all the countries (he visited) were but a trifle to him
	as he swiftly flew through them preaching the Gospel.
	Who like him ever gave of the labour of his hands for the Gospel?
	Night and day he supplied all its costs.[5]
25	He served the Gospel and it received its needs from him,
	lest for any reason its progress should be halted.
	What shepherd does not taste the milk of his flock[6]
	save this one, who was without blemish in his preaching?
	His is not merely a single virtue that one might talk about;
30	he strove after all the virtues and by his industry acquired them.
	"I am a prisoner of Jesus[7] and a servant of the Cross;
	pain, tiredness and nakedness have I learned from Him."
	He was persecuted by his own race,[8] those far off[9] and those close at hand;[10]
	full of love, he went hungry, was thirsty and he fasted.[11]

COMMENTARY OF GAL. 6:17 "FOR I CARRY THE MARKS OF JESUS BRANDED ON MY BODY."

35	He bore the marks of the Son of God[12] upon his limbs,
	and all the sufferings of the Crucified were imprinted on him.
	He was a necklace, rich with wounds as its adornments;
	in place of gems were inset the sufferings of the Son.
	He was a royal robe, dyed not in the blood of shellfish

---

[5] 1 Thess.1:9.
[6] 1 Cor. 9:7.
[7] Eph.3:1; Philem. 1:9.
[8] 2 Cor.11:24.
[9] Acts 24:23, 27.
[10] 2 Cor. 11:28.
[11] 2 Cor 11:28.
[12] Gal. 6:17.

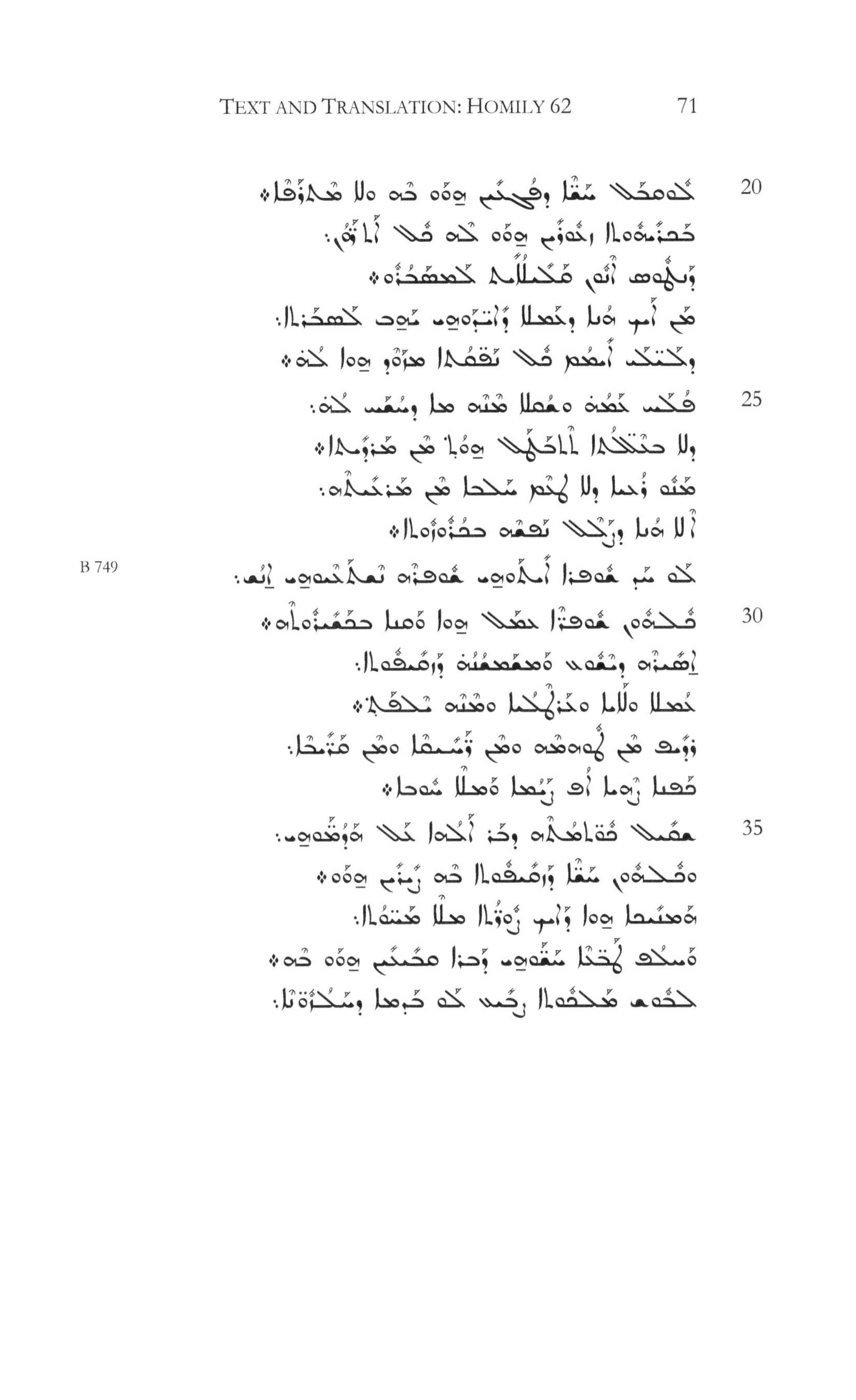

40	but in the blood of his very own lacerated body.
	Daily did the flick of the whip impress its mark;
	the Cross, like beryl, was etched upon his limbs.
	"I bear the marks of our Lord Jesus upon my body."[13]
	Who but this man ever displayed such splendours upon himself?
45	He bore the marks which were more glorious than any adornment;
	because of this there is no beauty like unto his.
	All the sufferings of the Son he fixed upon himself.
	I call him 'robe embroidered with sufferings'.
	He shone out with the marks he carried upon him;
50	the sun itself does not glow as fair as he.
	Come! Hear from him, whom this occasion has given to narrate his beauty,
	what jewels he boasts of to have on his crown:
	labour and vigil, not to mention blows and wounds,
	many an imprisonment and death and insults.
55	Five times was he scourged by the Jews,[14]
	three times was he beaten severely with rods.[15]
	Again, from his persecutors, a raincloud of stones fell upon him.[16]
	How astounding to hear the accounts of his suffering!

HUMILITY OF PAUL

Each day was a death, as he himself swore;[17]

---

[13] Gal. 6:17.
[14] 2 Cor. 11:24.
[15] 2 Cor. 11:25a.
[16] 2 Cor. 11:25b.
[17] 1 Cor. 15:31.

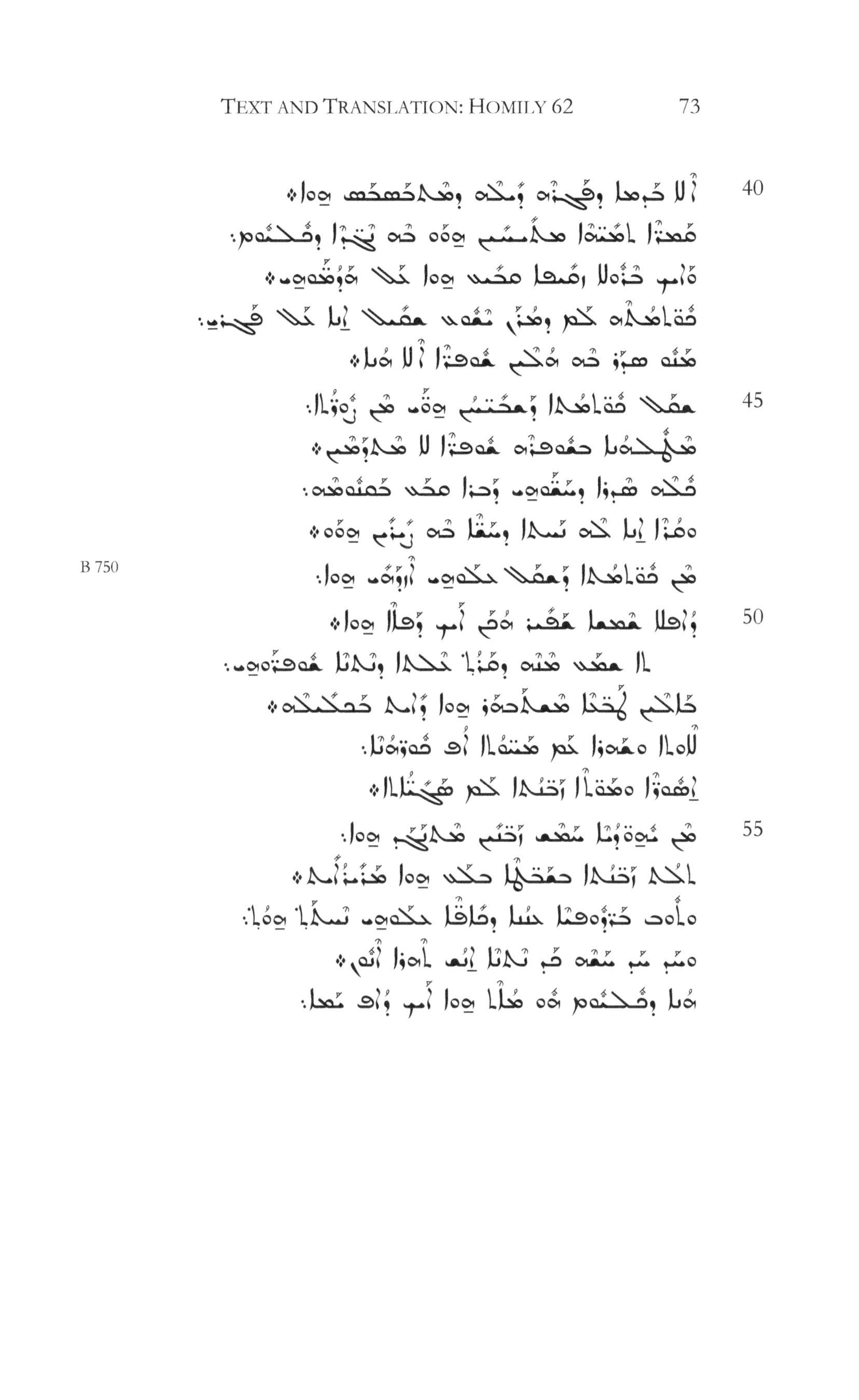

60	he carried the Cross and preached it all day long.
	He grew rich with visions and revelations;
	he understood the mysteries of creation better than Moses.
	He was caught up to the third heaven[18]
	and passing beyond, saw Paradise, as he told us.[19]
65	He heard the sublime voice of God
	that the mouth is neither allowed nor able to express.
	In his humility he did not disclose anything of what he saw,
	so that he might not boast while recounting his revelations.
	Fourteen years[20] he kept secret this mystery,
70	till need arose and only then did he tell it, as a means to an end.
	Who can match this man in humility,
	who did not glory in his revelations, marvelous as they were?
	He gazed at the humility of Jesus and humbled himself.
	No love of glory blustered wherever he was found.
75	From the Crucifixion's pigments he purloined his colours
	and portrayed himself after the likeness of the Son of God.
	The more he was raised up to the mysteries of the Son, the more he lowered and humbled himself,
	that he might arrive at the beauty of the humility of the Son.
	He addressed all his disciples with no other title than "my brothers"

---

[18] 2 Cor. 12:2.
[19] 2 Cor. 12:4.
[20] 2 Cor. 12:2.

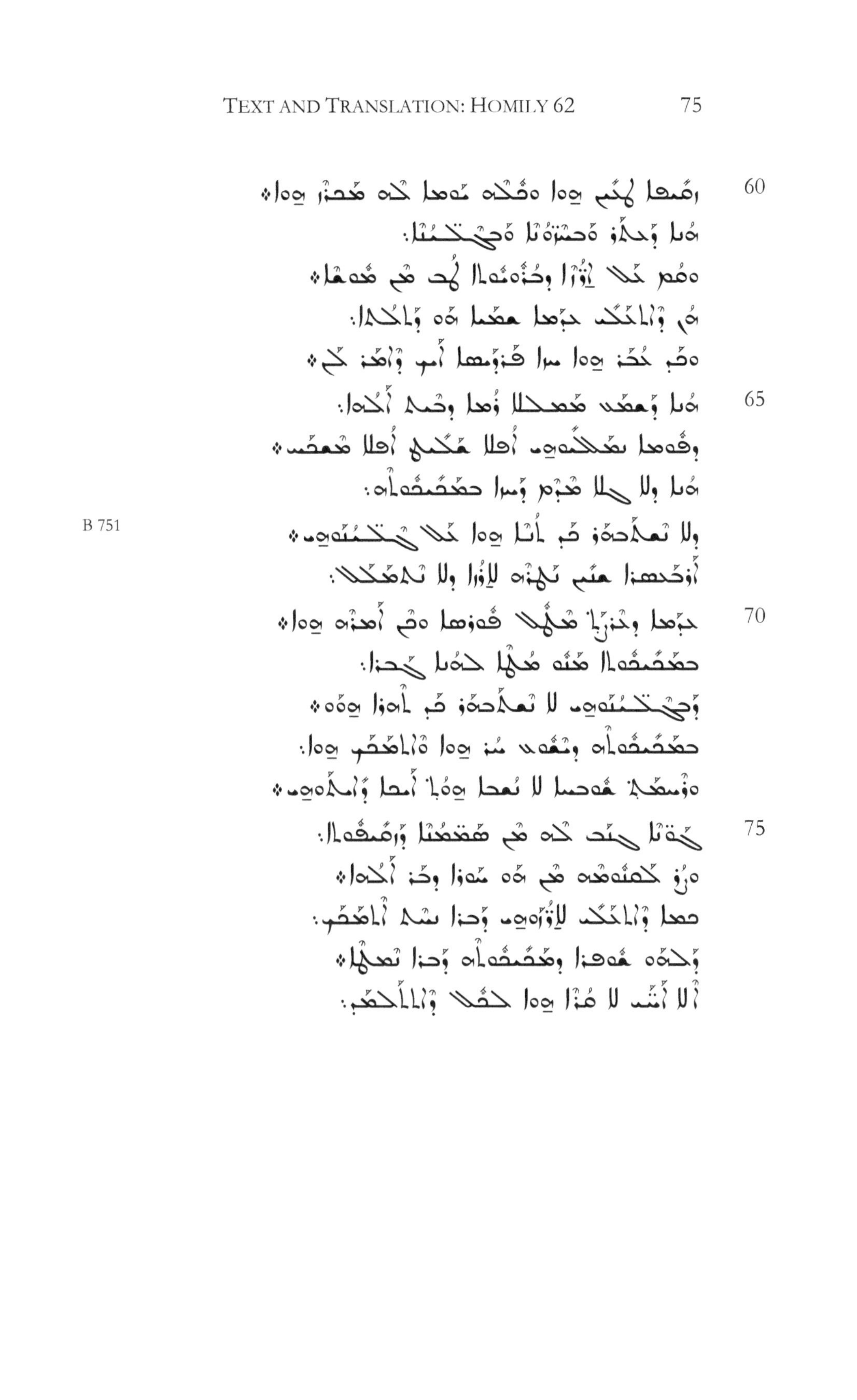

: B 751

80 because he only considered spiritual birth as genuine.
He disregarded the lineage in which he was born according to the flesh,
and pictured before himself that second birth, which is of the Spirit.
He did not regard Eve, but Baptism,
and he did not know who Adam was, but who Jesus was.
85 Therefore everyone who became his disciples he called "my brother,"
so that they might not remember the former state beyond which he had passed.

Commentary of Gal.6:17 "For I decided to know nothing among you except Jesus Christ, and Him crucified."

Who, like this man, while being wise, well-informed and educated,
could say that he did not believe in anything but the Crucified.[21]
"The Arameans[22] seek wisdom,
90 but I will not preach anything but Christ who was crucified[23] and slain."
While being the equal of the Arameans in wisdom,
he confined his theme to the simplicity of Jesus.
He limited his words to the scorn of the Cross,
without introducing clever artifice into his preaching.
95 He came to understand the great power of the Crucified;
he grasped that everyone would be subject to this Name.
He saw that the Cross is the leaven in which there is life
and he kneaded it into the dough of his apostleship.
With this message he lifted up his voice among the Nations,

---

[21] 1 Cor. 2:2.

[22] Aramean is a synonym for pagan. But in the New Testament it is translated as the Greeks.

[23] 1 Cor. 1:23.

TEXT AND TRANSLATION: HOMILY 62

B 752

100	as he preached nothing other than "The Cross! The Cross!"
	Here he concentrated all the power of his proclamation
	because he knew that all wisdom was herein contained.
	He said, "I will not display any wonders among the Jews,
	nor have I wisdom to speak among the Arameans.
105	I preach unto them Christ crucified,[24] a stumbling block and a scandal,[25]
	because He is the end of all wisdom and wonders."
	The Cross became a teacher to Paul and he learnt from it,
	to forget his education and become simple by faith.
	He was taught to retrace his steps and forget everything he had learned;
110	it (the Cross) bid him to become unlettered, and then to be received.
	This is the schooling of the Cross: sheer simplicity!
	Whoever is wise, let him forget (his wisdom), then he will learn.
	Therefore Paul rejected worldly instruction,
	to be enlightened by simplicity.
115	He learned to speak only of Christ crucified,
	for He is the totality of true teaching.
	Wherever it be found, truth is wiser than all things;
	even an uneducated person, when speaking it, is as clear as the sun.
	When Paul preached, he was scrupulous concerning the truth

---

[24] 1 Cor. 1:22–23.
[25] Rom. 9:33.

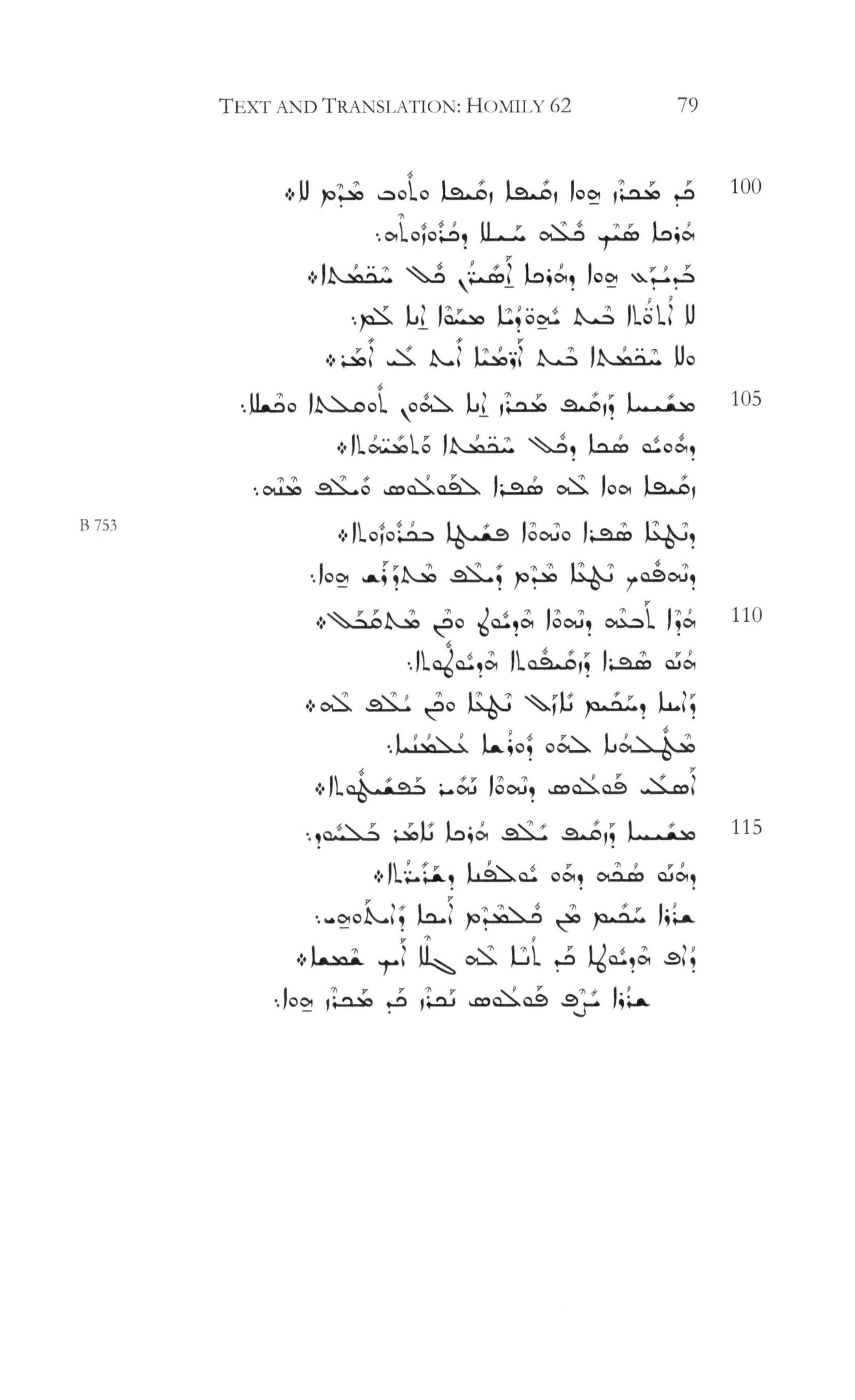

B 753

120	and so he never said pretentious things to make himself appear wise.
	He was a vision full of wonder to all who looked upon him: men and angels alike were in awe of him.

COMMENTARY OF I COR.4:9 "…WE HAVE BECOME A SPECTACLE TO THE PEOPLE AND TO ANGELS."

	"We have become a spectacle to people and to angels":[26]
	he became for the whole world a show that it beheld with wonder.
125	Though his body was bound, his word made speed throughout the lands.
	Though he was cast into chains, his writings stirred up the earth.
	His hands were shackled, yet his voice was very rich in proclamation;
	they beat him yet he bore it, as he said.
	They cursed him, but he blessed them with kindness;
130	they persecuted him and he entreated them, and he will tell you.[27]
	In one place he suffered dishonor and he did not murmur;
	in another, they honored him and he would not accept it.
	In one place they honored him with a bull as though he were a god;[28]
	in another, they dragged him ruthlessly to the ground as though he were a dog.[29]
135	On one occasion they called him Hermes and he reprimanded them;[30]
	on another, they considered him insane and he accepted them.[31]
	He was considered to be both misleading and true;
	he was poor, yet made many rich.[32]
	Look at him one moment plying his trade at tent-making,

---

[26] 1 Cor. 4:9.
[27] 1 Cor. 4:11–13.
[28] Acts 14:13.
[29] Acts 14:19.
[30] Acts 14:12.
[31] Acts 26:24.
[32] 1 Cor. 6:8, 10.

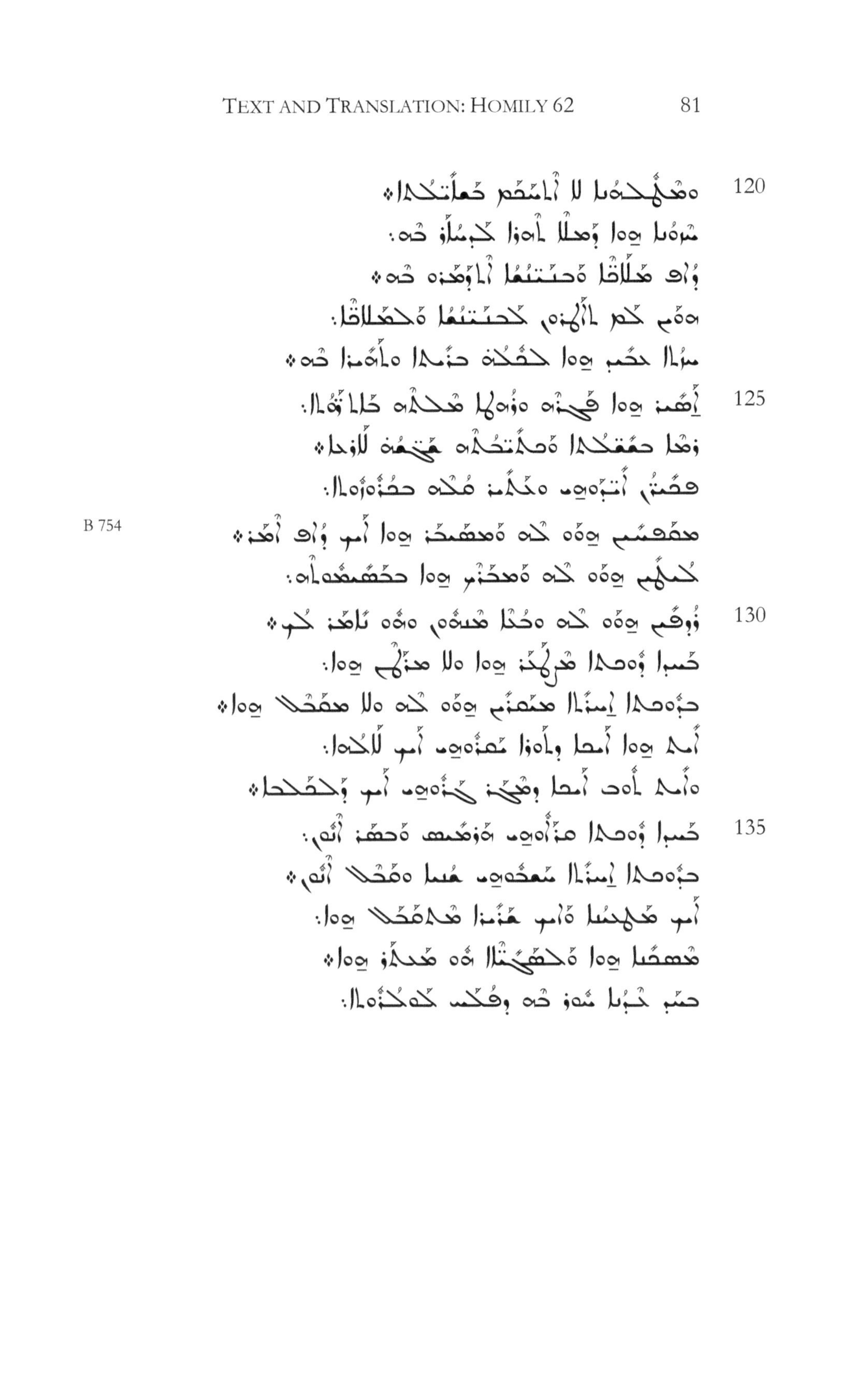

B 754

140 and the next, performing mighty works and miracles;
in one place shut up in prison as a murderer;
in another, restoring life to a youth after a fall.[33]
If it is fetters you seek, they were put upon him;
if remedies for the afflicted, they are found in him.
145 On one occasion, for convenience sake, he (said he) was a Roman;[34]
and again, when it was necessary, he disclosed to the council that he was a Pharisee.[35]
His 'lying' was full of truth and he was not lying;
by means fair and fowl he devised ways to increase the Gospel.
Go to the city wall and see him being let down in a basket; [36]
150 then look to heaven, as he goes up in a revelation.
Listen as he threatens to take up the rod when necessary;[37]
then come and see as they stone him, and he is not furious.[38]
In one place he called himself "the scum of the world";[39]
in another, an "Israelite" and "a son of Abraham".[40]
155 He proceeded in succession upon both greatness and littleness.
While being great he humbled himself like his Master.
Yes, for sure, he was a wondrous spectacle full of visions
and both angels and men stood astonished at him.
They saw him full of anger persecuting Jesus;

---

[33] Acts 20:9–12.
[34] Cf. Chapter 16 and 22 of the Acts of the Apostles.
[35] Acts 23:6.
[36] Acts 9:25.
[37] 1 Cor. 4:21.
[38] Acts 14:19.
[39] 1 Cor. 4:13.
[40] Rom. 11:1; 2 Cor. 11:22.

TEXT AND TRANSLATION: HOMILY 62

B 755

160   they looked again and beheld him persecuted in every place for His sake.
Some days earlier he stoned the proto-martyr in his zeal;[41]
a few days later he too is stoned, and he put up with it.
He was as wily as a serpent when it came to disputation
but as innocent as a dove in the teaching of the Cross.[42]
165   Where he wanted, he outwitted philosophers in debate;
and where he preferred (he said), "We are fools for Christ."[43]
All his life he was lifted up by sufferings
and was revived by beatings as by appetizing foods.
Nothing gladdened him so much as sufferings:
170   "I rejoice in the sufferings I have borne for you."[44]
Who like him ever rejoiced in his own sufferings as he rejoiced?
I am amazed by him; I am unable to tell his story.
"I rejoice in these sufferings for your sake."[45]
Explain this to us so we can see why you rejoice!

COMMENTARY OF COL. I:24 "I AM FILLING UP WHAT IS LACKING IN ALL THE SUFFERINGS OF CHRIST IN BODY FOR THE SAKE OF THE CHURCH WHICH IS HIS BODY."

175   "I am filling up what is lacking in all the sufferings of Christ in my body
for the sake of the Church which is His body.[46]
Look! In the place of Jesus I am ready to receive with joy
every suffering for the Church's sake.
He is in heaven and does not die or suffer;

---

[41] Acts 7:58–8:1.
[42] Mt. 10:16.
[43] 1 Cor. 4:10.
[44] Col. 1:23.
[45] Col. 1:24.
[46] Ibid.

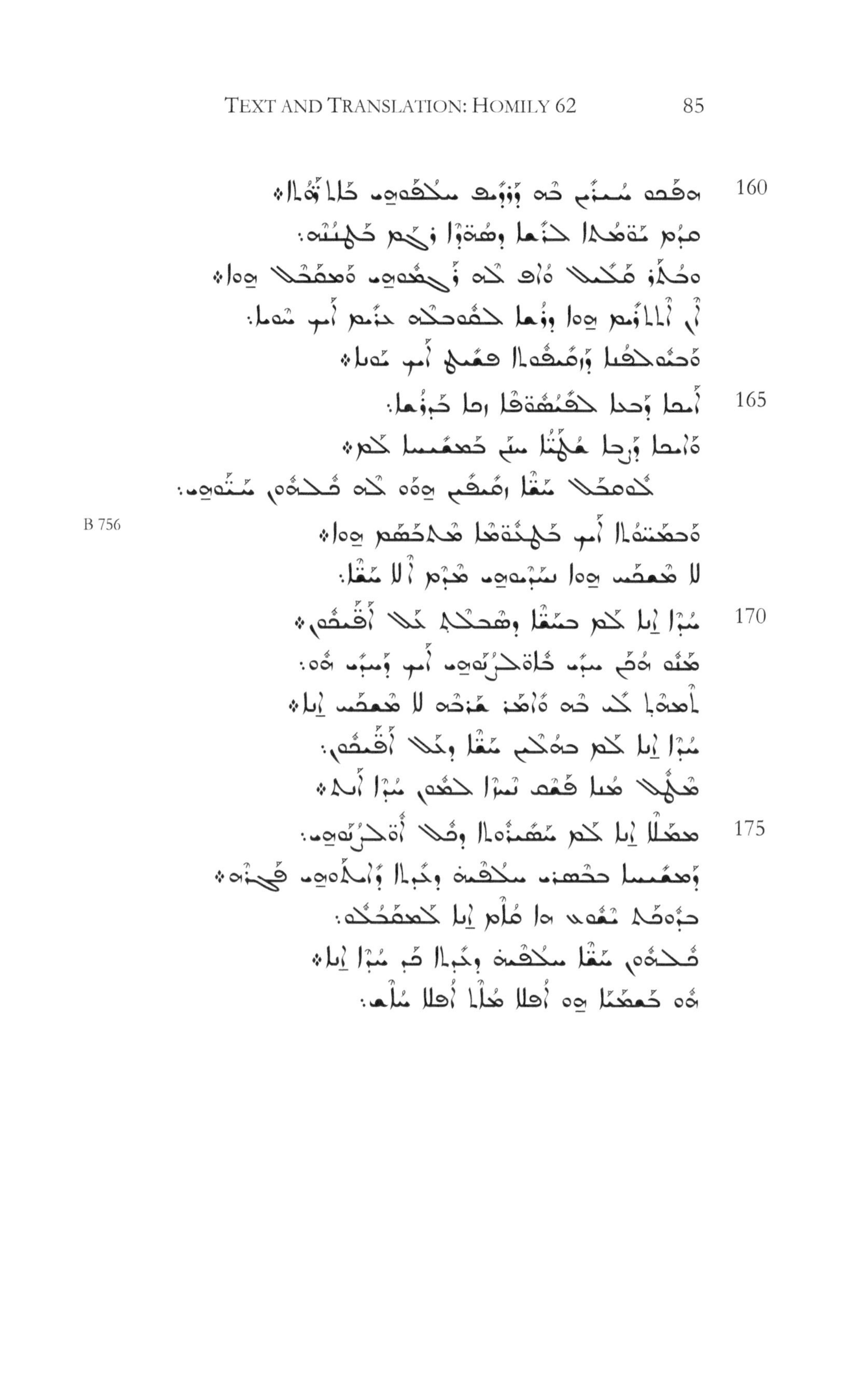

B 756

180	I fill up His place that I might be struck by the persecutors.
	He who seeks to strike Jesus, let him come and strike me;
	whoever is roused in anger against Him, let him assuage his anger on me.
	If there is someone who threatens Him, behold here I stand:
	let him heap all possible sufferings upon me; I accept them.
185	If there is any suffering that Jesus did not endure for His Church,
	I will fill up whatever is lacking in all His sufferings.
	I am ready and happy to undergo all manner of sufferings,
	for the sake of His body, which is His Church.
	If the crucifiers still harbor any murderous malice,
190	let it melt away in me as I endure every suffering.
	If any bitterness of the priests continues to fester, let it be emptied out on me,
	that the lack in the sufferings of the Son may be fulfilled in me.
	If out of jealousy an arrow is drawn against the Church,
	let it not strike her, but pierce my flesh as I take delight.
195	If fury is stirred up against her (the Church) by judges,
	I will enter (the courtroom) and have all the punishments meted out upon me.
	If the rulers of the world threaten her with their power,
	I will stand to endure the pain that she may not be hurt.
	If the anger of kings is stirred up against her who is pure,

TEXT AND TRANSLATION: HOMILY 62

B 757

200	then let all fury on her account be poured upon me.
	I will fulfill in my flesh what is lacking in all sufferings,
	that the Church of the Son be preserved from all harm.
	Of all earthly people, who has ever loved Christ like him?
	Who can attain this measure, which is immeasurable?
205	Who has ever consented to endure such suffering for so many,
	except he that took it upon him gladly?
	On whom was such boldness ever bestowed,
	to fulfill what is lacking in the sufferings of the Son, though He lacks nothing?
	"I rejoice in these sufferings which are for you,
210	and I fulfill what is lacking in the sufferings of the Son."[47]
	He desired to receive in his body all the blows
	that were aimed on every side against the Church.
	When the envy of rulers was barking at the Church,
	he assented that it should bite him so that she might remain unhurt.
215	All the waves that rose menacingly against the Church,
	he was happy and prepared to have them strike him.
	He perceived the beauty of the sufferings of the Cross,
	and so he greatly rejoiced in every suffering.
	He taught the Church who He is, and whose Son it is who died for her,

---

[47] Ibid.

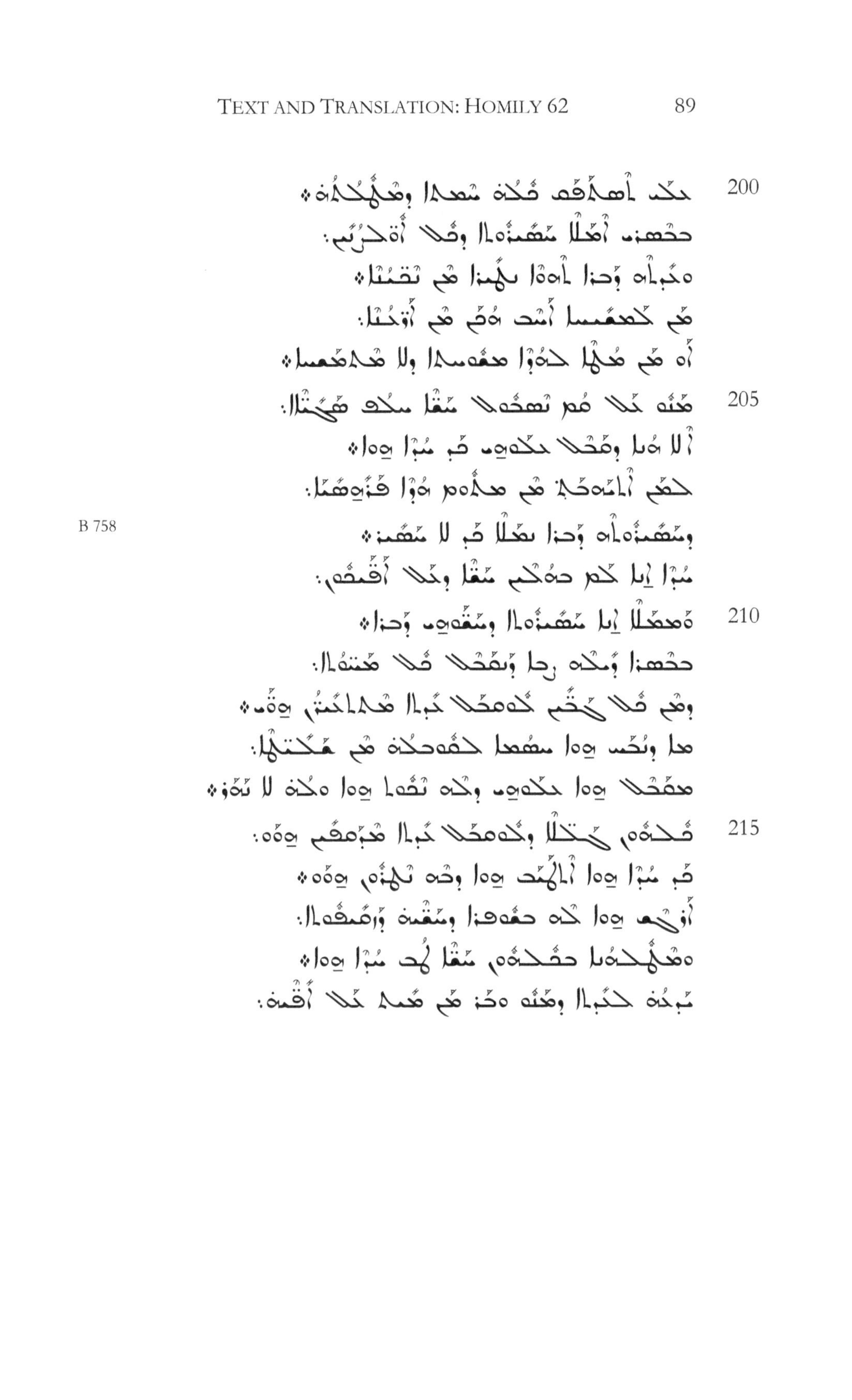

B 758

220	and while he endured suffering for her, he did not complain.
	He looked towards God, who purchased her by His own blood, as it is written,[48]
	and was ready to give himself on her behalf.
	The mind is unequal to his praises, for he is full of every beauty.
	It cannot grasp him so as to depict his image from any viewpoint.
225	It is not so much that discourse is slow to look and depict his likeness
	but that he presses swiftly on, and his beauty cannot be captured.
	He said, "I press on that I may make my own
	that for which Christ has made me His own[49] when He came for our sakes."
	Paul pressed on unceasingly in his apostolic office;
230	he flew to all the nations with the Gospel, succeeding again and again.
	Every road and every place was filled up by him;
	he did not slow down to take a rest and then resume his course.
	So swift was he in his course that he did not like to look behind:

COMMENTARY OF PHIL. 3:13 "I FORGET THOSE THINGS WHICH ARE BEHIND ME BECAUSE THEY ARE IN THE PAST AND I STRAIN FORWARD AS MUCH AS I CAN TOWARDS WHAT LIES AHEAD OF ME."

	"I forget what lies behind me and I strain forward to what is before me."[50]
235	After winning over one place on the circuit of his preaching,
	he put it behind him and went on to the next so that he might toil there also.
	He did not care to sit down and ponder on yesterday's labour
	but rather pressed on to complete the task of today.
	Yesterday they stoned him, and he forgets yesterday's sufferings;

---

[48] Acts 20:28.
[49] Phil. 3:12.
[50] Phil. 3:13.

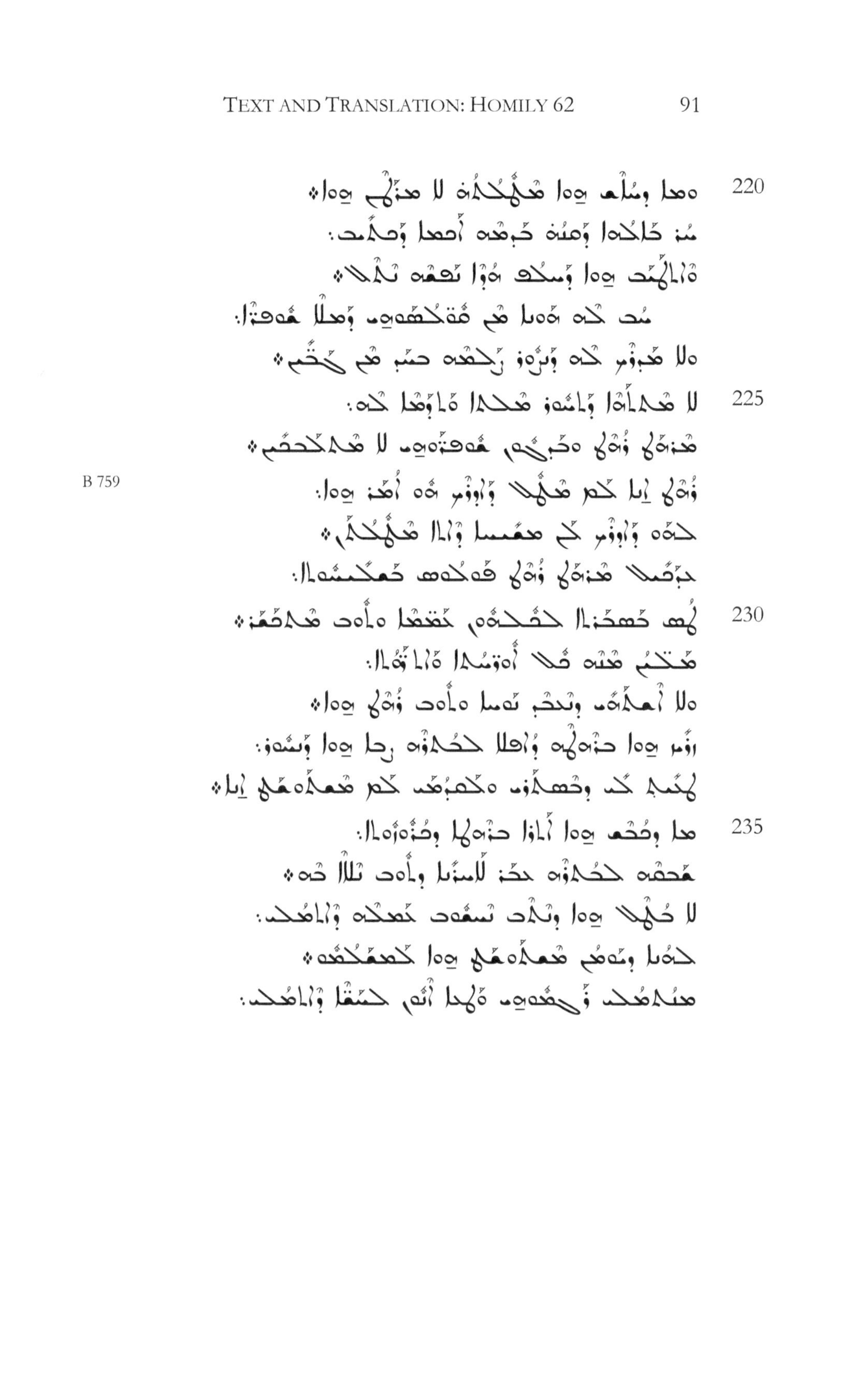

240	today he seeks out yet more sufferings to endure.
	"I forget those things which are behind me because they are in the past,
	and I strain forward as much as I can towards what lays ahead of me."
	He did not brood over a travail that slipped away with the close of day
	but took pains to work on what was present.
245	It is loathsome to a lion to eat yesterday's prey;
	daily he seeks to hunt what befits the day.
	Thus Paul passed on from labour done in error,
	and strove to approach what lay ahead.
	There is no place that was not taken by him in the course that he set himself;
250	though he achieved much, he pressed on all the more, to attain the more.
	Where should discourse look for him, to narrate his beautiful deeds?
	In what place shall a homily grasp him, if indeed it does so?
	He was driven forward on every road, and entire countries were not enough for him;
	I do not know where I may catch him, to depict his beauties.
255	While I seek to hear his voice from Rome,
	news comes to me that he is thrown to the beasts in Ephesus.[51]
	While listening to the sound of his speech in Syria,
	I turn and hear that he has converted Galatia.
	When I seek to catch sight of his beauty from Corinth,

---

[51] 1 Cor. 15:32.

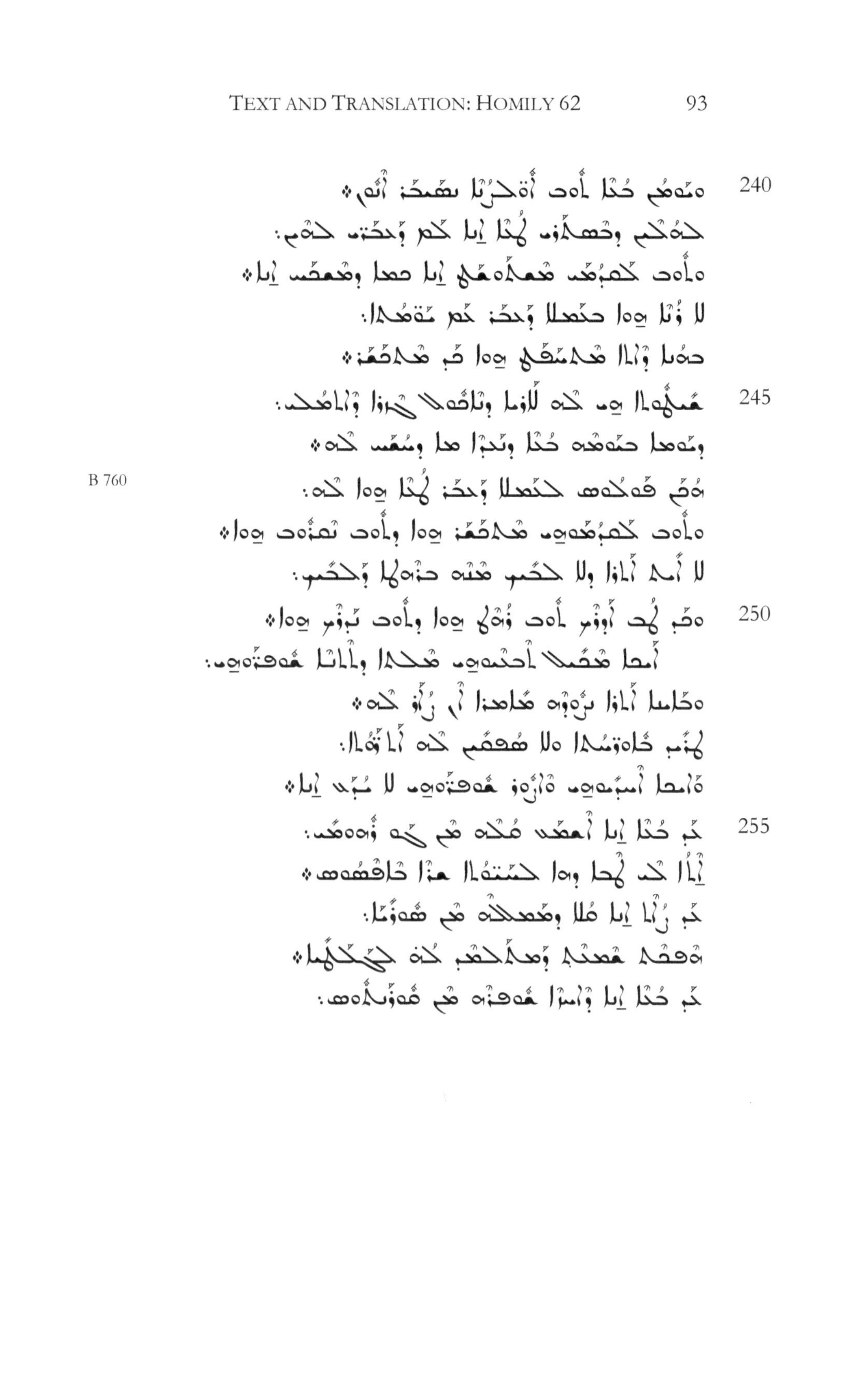

260	he shows himself to me from Jerusalem with the saints.
	If go to the sea, I see him shipwrecked,
	and on dry land, in shackles, yet going about his preaching.
	He admonishes Cephas[52] and restrains an angel by his imprecation;[53]
	he is circumspect in the Gospel lest it be spoken in a careless manner.
265	When it is expedient, he becomes like a Jew to the Jews;[54]
	and when it is necessary, he lives as one outside the Law.[55]
	He took pains, as he said, to win over all people;[56]
	his truth was one yet he conducted himself differently according to circumstances.
	When he was preaching he was a partner with the Spirit in his words;
270	but when admonishing, he was on his own; it was not from the Spirit.
	"I speak, not the Lord."[57] Here he showed
	that even when not commanded, he admonished and corrected as best he could.
	As long as the Spirit commanded him to speak, behold, he spoke;
	and when the Spirit left him to take a little rest, he did not let up.
275	Because of this he wrote to Timothy,
	"Admonish in season and out of season,[58] and do not cease."
	This hard-worker had no time to stop and be still,
	for there was never a time that he was not engaged in business to make a profit.
	"For three years I admonished with tears night and day."[59]

---

[52] Gal. 2:11.
[53] Gal. 1:8–9.
[54] 1 Cor. 9:20a.
[55] 1 Cor. 9:20b.
[56] 1 Cor. 9:20–22.
[57] 1 Cor. 7:12.
[58] 2 Tim. 4:2.
[59] Acts 20:31.

| | 260
| |
| |
| |
| |
| | 265
| |
| |
B 761 | |
| |
| | 270
| |
| |
| |
| |
| | 275
| |
| |
| |
| |

280	Who has ever wept so long without being comforted?
	At that time iniquity was laid out like a corpse;
	for three years he wept and admonished, and then he buried it.
	Until he had enshrouded the iniquity and buried it, he would not be comforted,
	since, as long it lived, he was pained to see it.
285	For all that I might say, I cannot tell of any of his praises,
	but should I keep silent, I cannot hold off from that steadfast man.
	My discourse gives no glory to that humble man;
	his glory is his own; is it not from his mind?
	His mind bore witness to him, and it is a marvel
290	that someone is not to be accused by himself in anything at all.
	This man was not aware of anything against himself,[60]
	and so he was blessed, for he did not judge there to be any cause of condemnation in himself.
	The depths of this homily (on Paul) have overwhelmed me now,
	and I can neither climb out nor rescue myself by staying silent.
295	So, like him, I will cry out, "O the depths![61]
	No one can search the beauties that are hidden within you!"
	So much was he intoxicated with the love of the Son of God
	that he even sought to become a stranger to Him for His love's sake.
	Here we must prepare ourselves to hear in a different way,

---

[60] 1 Cor. 4:4.
[61] Rom. 11:33.

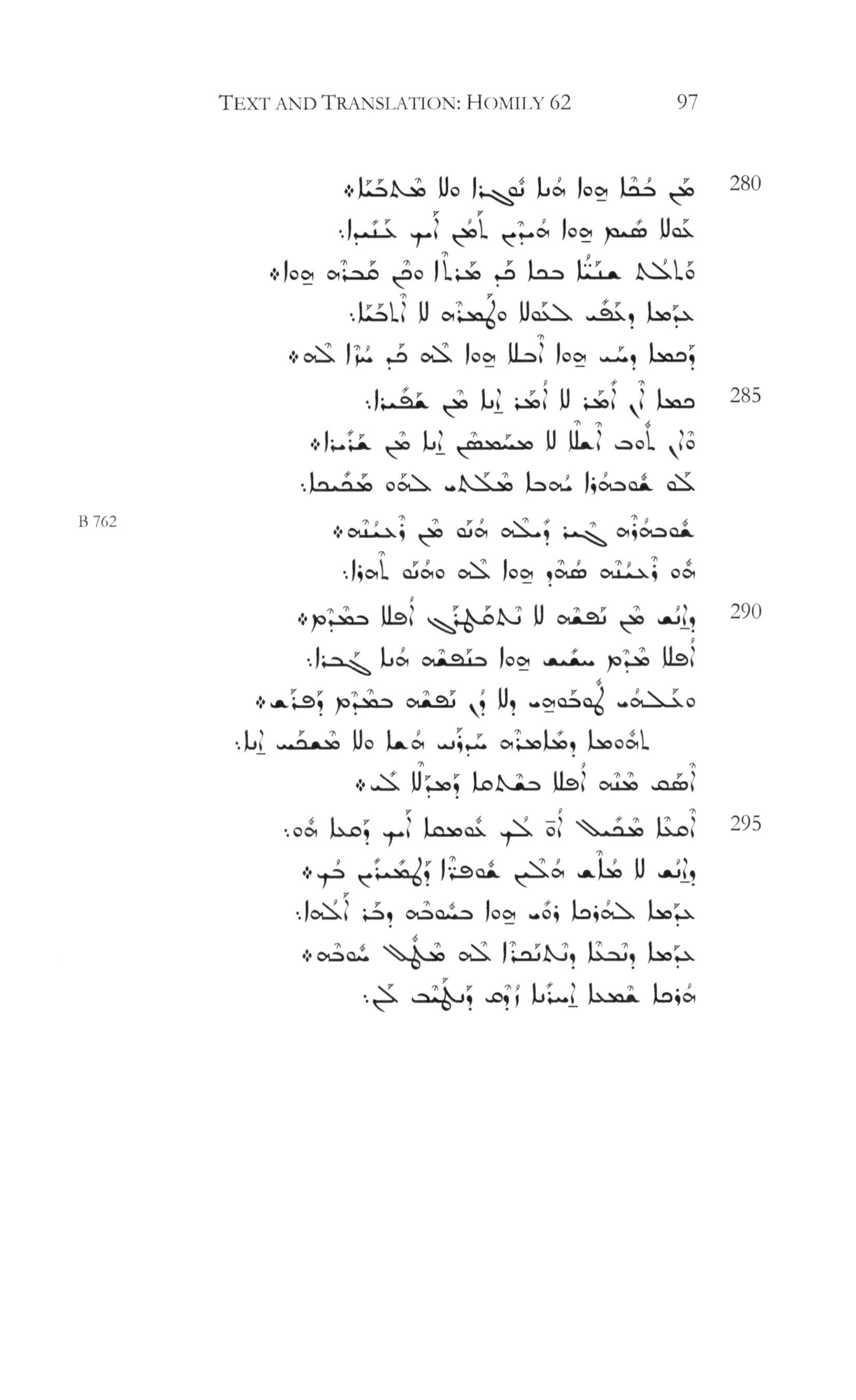

for the thing I speak about is not of the natural order.

COMMENTARY OF ROM 9:3 "I HAVE PRAYED THAT I MYSELF WERE ACCURSED FOR ISRAEL'S SAKE SO THAT IT MAY NOT BE ESTRANGED FROM ITS SAVIOUR."

"I have prayed that I myself were accursed[62] for Israel's sake,
so that it may not be estranged from its Saviour."
Here the level of discourse exceeds all ability to hear.
The hearing of the ear and the apprehension of the mind cannot contain it.
What measure has enough space for words such as these,
that someone should pray to be accursed from God?
It was not because he hated God that he sought to be accursed from Him,
but rather that he loved Him intensely.
Love of the Son burned greater in that man than any fire,
to such an extent that his love even compelled him to be accursed.
See how ardent he was in the love of God when he spoke these words,
and how strongly persuaded that he could not be separated from it.
"Who shall separate me from the love of God?
Shall tribulation, or distress, or perhaps famine?[63]
I am persuaded that neither death, nor life,
nor angels, nor princes, nor powers,[64]
nor things present, nor things to come in their varied forms,
neither height, nor depth nor anything in them,[65]
nor any other possible created thing can separate from God

---

[62] Rom. 9:3.
[63] Rom. 8:35.
[64] Rom. 8:38.
[65] Rom. 8:39.

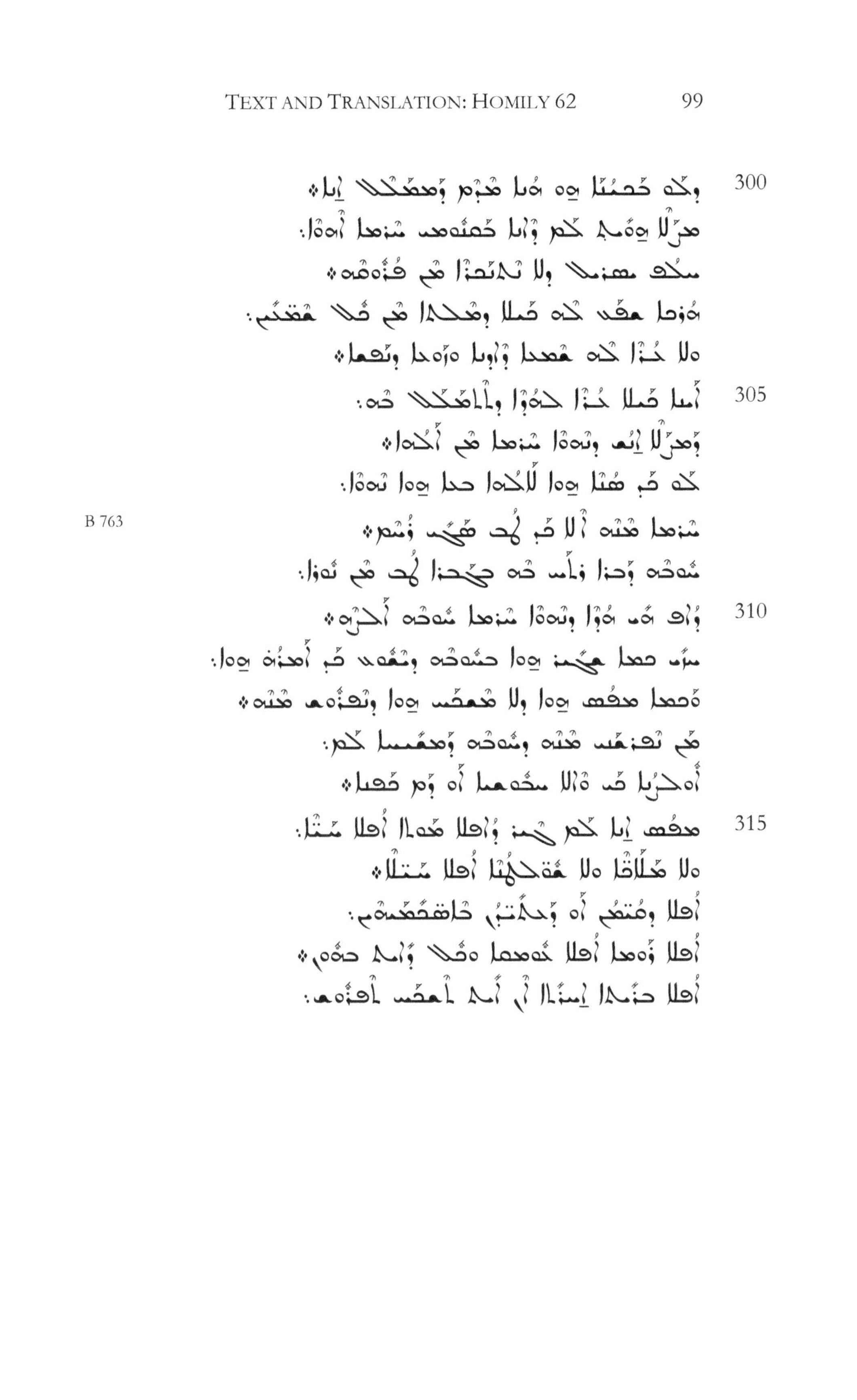

 B 763

320	my love that is in our Lord Jesus Christ."[66]
	Since he was bound fast by the love of God and inseparable from it,
	why did he pray to be accursed, if not because of that love?
	Death, life, angels, and powers,
	Paul showed to be smaller than his mind.
325	"Height, depth and all the orders in between,
	should they come against me, shall not separate me from God.
	No other possible creation, even if it did exist,
	would have power in it capable of separating my love from Him."
	Why this reference to any "other creation" – since it did not exist,
330	except to extend the measure of his love above every limit?
	"No other world," even if it were to come into being
	and exist alongside those that do exist, could separate me from God.
	By his word he passed beyond nature and its elements,
	pitching his argument high above nature to speak it there.
335	The whole creation was not enough for him to speak of,
	so he went beyond it, to another non-existent creation, to speak.
	He weighed all worlds against his love for God;
	all creation weighed less, and his love outweighed them all.
	Because of this he said, "No other world,

---

[66] Rom. 8:38–39.

︙

340	if it did exist, could separate me from Him."
	Since this is the case, I have prayed that I might be accursed
	for the sake of those who are lost, that they might be found in God.
	This is a big claim, and he is not to be blamed who cannot hear it,
	for the door of the ear is too small for it to fit through.
345	Bearing in mind the love Paul had towards God,
	what was the significance of his praying to be accursed from God?
	O Paul, your story surpasses all interpretation!
	Why did you pray to be accursed by your Beloved?
	If all worlds, as you said, cannot separate you,
350	why then do you pray to withdraw from Him.
	If things neither present nor to come will separate your love,
	why are you at pains to be separated, as you say?
	Unless you listen a little in a spiritual manner,
	the words of Paul will lie hidden from your understanding.
355	He looked to Jesus, who for our sake was made to be sin,[67]
	and he made himself ready to become accursed for His sake.
	The Son of God died on behalf of all,
	and Paul likewise sought to become accursed on behalf of many.
	He looked to God, and how much He loves people, (and he exclaimed)

---

[67] 2 Cor. 5:21.

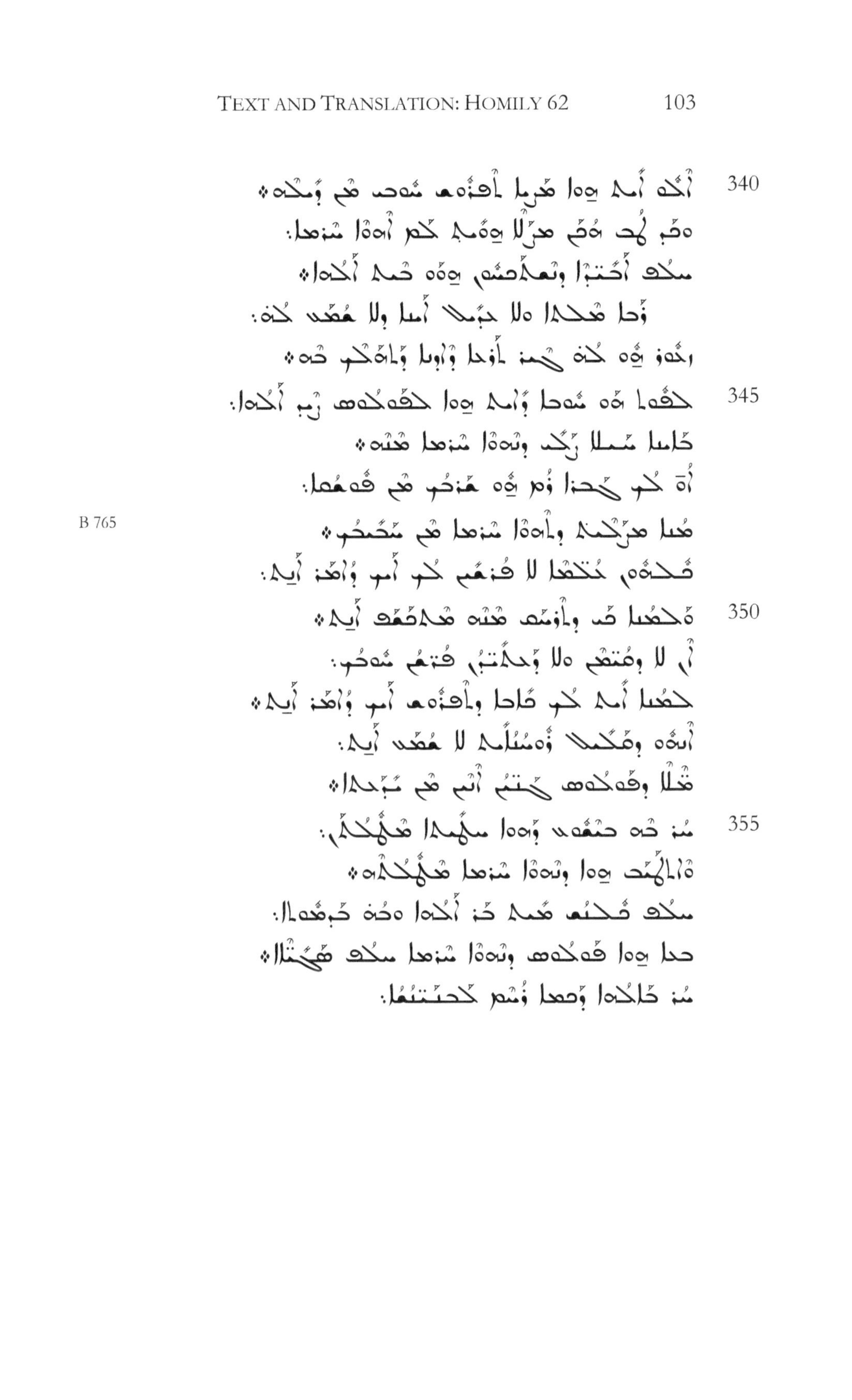

360	"I have wished to be accursed that they may be found."[68]
	That the way of the Son might not be made void,
	he prayed that he might be lost, and that the Son of God visit His own.
	He thought about Abraham and about the promises of the Father,
	and he was in pain, lest the covenant be rendered ineffective.[69]
365	He remembered the promises (given) to the fathers,
	but saw their offspring were at enmity with the Saviour.
	He read in the old covenant that they are sons in truth
	and was desperately saddened lest they forfeit their inheritance.
	He called to mind the glory in which they stood,
370	and the Law and Worship that they possessed.
	He understood how great were the covenants God had made,
	and how necessary that His word be established among His heirs.
	He pondered on Christ who was born of them according to the flesh,
	and was greatly pained lest they be deprived of this salvation.
375	"For the sake of these things lest they be rendered void,
	I have prayed to be accursed for them.
	Let me go out, and let them enter in unto God,
	That the great way of the Crucifixion be filled up.
	It is nothing, if for the sake of many, one person departs,

---

[68] Rom. 9:3.
[69] Rom. 9:4ff.

TEXT AND TRANSLATION: HOMILY 62 105

B 766

380 for the way of the Son is large enough for everybody, though few enter it.
I will go away; let them come to repentance,
and I will greatly rejoice if I am lost while they are found."
For these reasons Paul swore that he was in pain and distress
and prayed to be accursed.

LOVE OF PAUL FOR JESUS

385 Who is able to love, as he loved,
both God and neighbor more than himself?
The goal of Love and of the Law is this:
"You should love your neighbor as yourself."[70]
Paul loved beyond the goal of all love,
390 for not "as himself" only did he love, but far more.
He did not (merely) seek the advantage of others,
but that he should be lost and others be found.
He prayed to be at enmity with God that they might be reconciled,
and that he go out, so that the entire Nation be brought in.
395 No love is to be compared with this love,
except that of Jesus, who died for the wicked, and in whom they regained life.
Paul's rank is higher than all heights,
and however high I would scale to speak of him, I reach but the lowest rung.
Once something is under confinement, it remains confined;

---

[70] Mt. 22:39; Mk. 12:31.

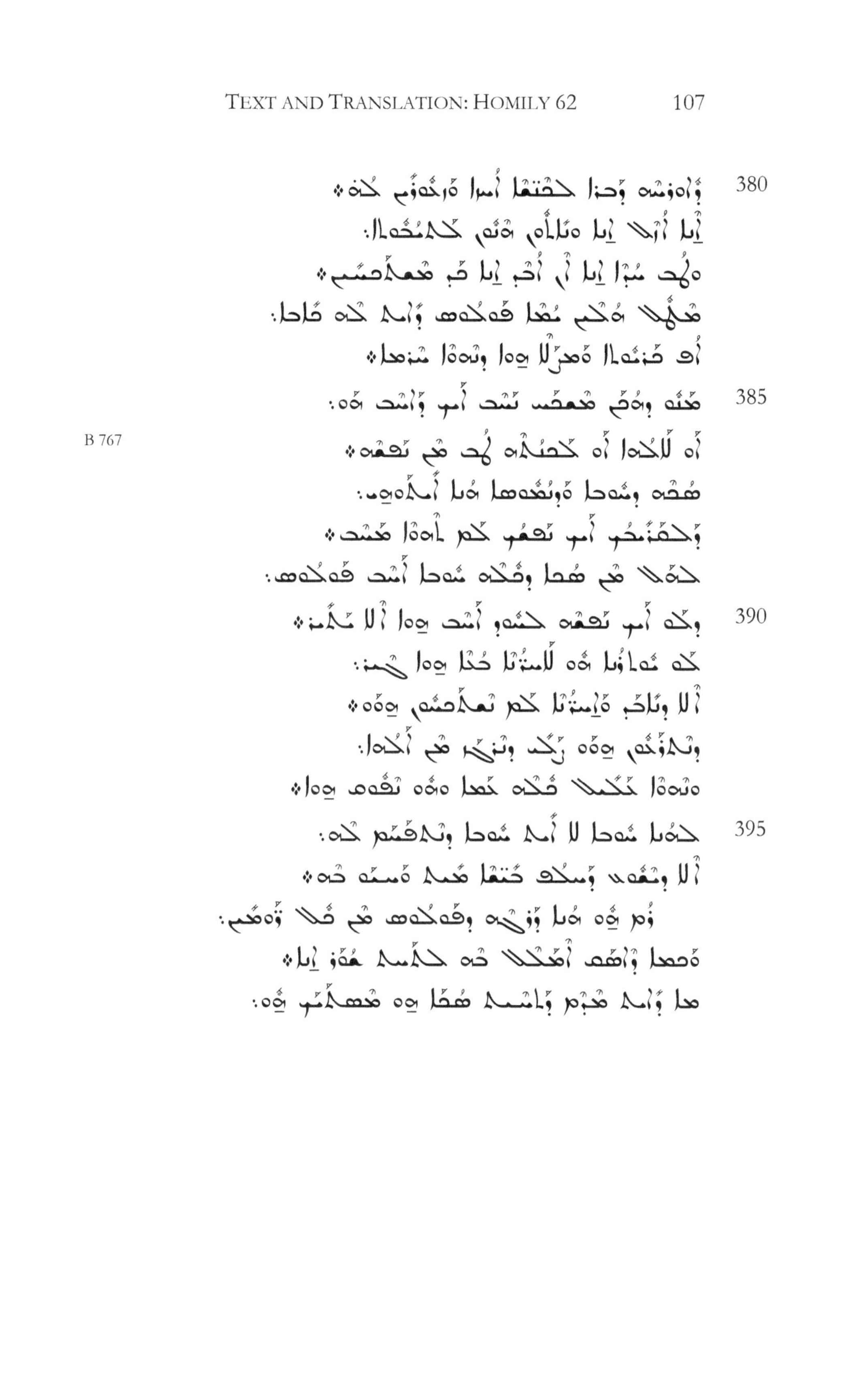

400	no matter how great it is, insofar as it is confined, it is not great.
	The story of Paul has neither confinement nor limit,
	and so is too great to be spoken of by my mouth.
	Look! I haven't said a word yet about his beauty:
	do not fault me for having said I would speak about that!
405	I wanted to speak, but wasn't up to the task, much as I desired.
	Beauty like this is not to be spattered with the colours from our palette.
	Therefore I will spread out silence like a veil to cover it,
	lest the jumble of my words, for all their enthusiasm, deface everything.
	Up to now I knew I was dealing with something that knows no boundaries,
410	but from now on I will say no more, lest I incur disgrace.
	I am not falling silent because I have lost the power of speech;
	in truth I confess I am not able to <speak>.
	Let me keep silent and let him speak, as is proper,
	and I will learn from him what crown he received in the Gospel.
415	"I have fought the good fight; I have finished the race;[71]
	I have kept my faith steadfast from stumbling blocks,
	and there is laid up in righteousness a crown for my Lord to give me,"
	for he judged of himself that he was to receive a crown in righteousness.[72]
	Paul became his own judge, and passed judgment,

---

[71] 2 Tim. 4:7.
[72] 2 Tim. 4:8.

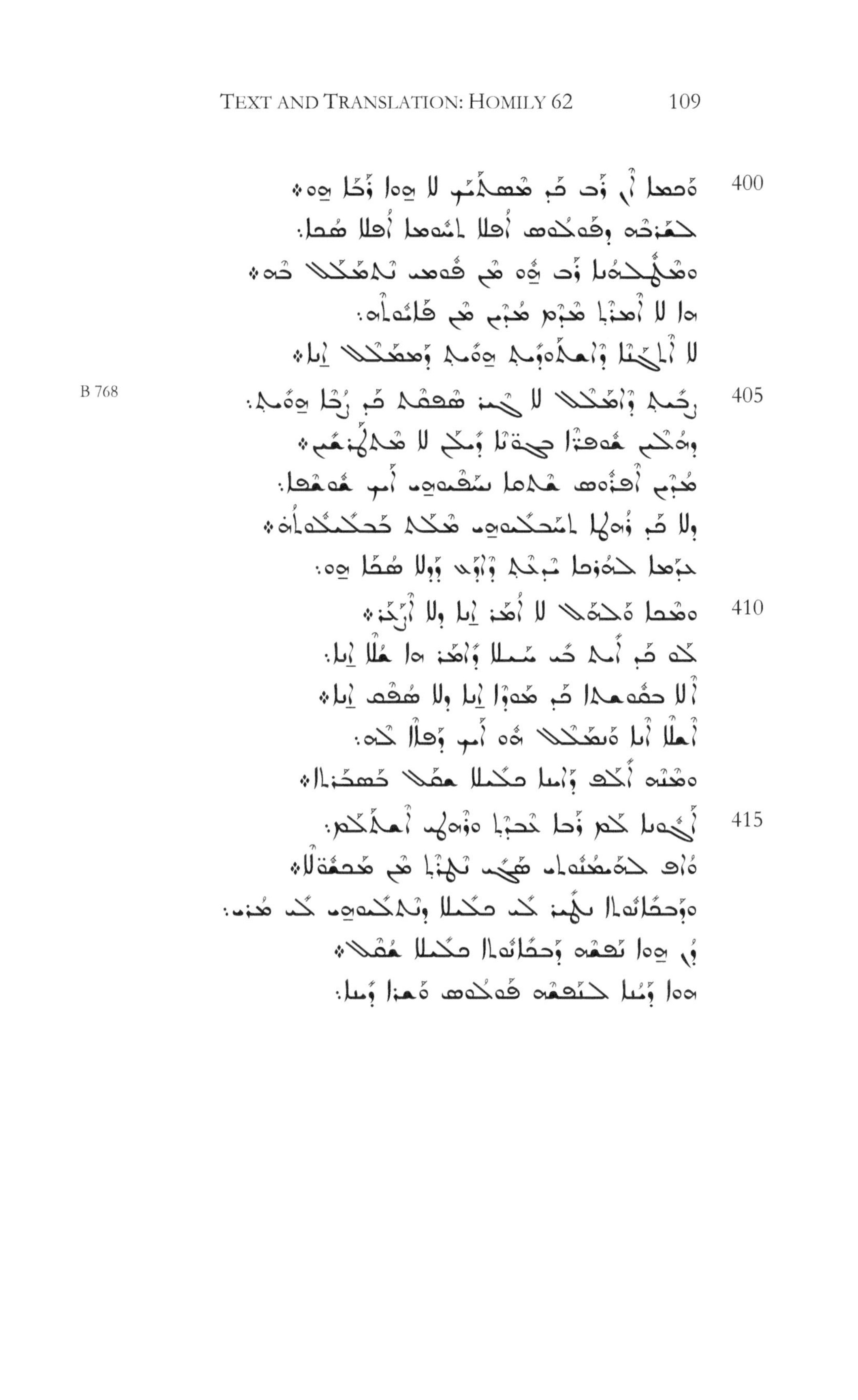

420 that a crown was kept for him in righteousness from God.
He summoned his thoughts to be witnesses to his deeds
and all of them exclaimed, "You lack nothing but the crown."
Rightly did the Learned One (Jesus) call him "a chosen vessel."[73]
424 Blessed is He who kept for him the crown of victory of which he was worthy. Amen.
The end of the second homily on the Apostle Paul
composed by Mar Jacob Malpan.

---

[73] Acts 9:15.

420

ܘܲܚܕܵܐܝܼܐܝܼܬ݂ ܒܲܝܢܵܬ݂ ܟܠܗ ܥܠܡܐ ܡܢ ܐܟܘܬܗ܀
ܗܕܐ ܠܫܲܡܘܼܥܲܘܗܝ ܘܢܗܘܘܢ ܗܲܘܪܵܐ ܠܟܠ ܦܘܕܵܪ̈ܝܵܬ݂ܗܘܢ܂
ܕܡܢܗ ܕܘܼܟܬܗ ܘܐܠܐ ܥܠܡܐ ܠܐ ܡܫܟܲܚ ܐܢܫ܀

B 769

ܗܟܢ ܗܘܒ݂ܝ ܗܢܐ ܢܚܡܐ ܗܢܝܚ ܗܢܘܗܝ ܒܪܘܚܐ.
ܕܐܝܟ ܘܒܠܝܢ ܟܠܗ ܥܠܡܐ ܐܢܕܡܐ ܘܗܘܐ ܒܘܼܐ ܠܗ܀

ܗܢܘ ܗܘܐܢܐ (ܗܐܪܙܢ؟) ܘܟܠܐ ܩܘܕܘܗ ܥܠܡܢܐ:
ܘܐܚܢܢ ܠܩܕܡ ܢܩܼܘܡܝ ܡܕܠܢܐ.

BIBLIOGRAPHY OF WORKS CITED

Acharya, F. *Prayer with the Harp of the Spirit*, Vol 1–6. Vagamon, 1982–86.

Anto, J. "Revelation of Paul the Blessed Apostle," *The Harp* XII (2007): 269–282.

Assemani, J.S. *Bibliothecae Apostolicae Vaticanae*. Vol.III, pp.87–107 (Rome, 1759).

Auweele, B.V. *From Babel to the Upper Room*. Translation and Interpretation of Homilies of Narsai and Jacob of Serug. Louvain-la-Neuve, 2001.

Baumstark, A. *Geschicte der syrischen Literatur mit Ausschluss der christlich-palastinensischen Texte*. Bonn, 1922.

——— "Die Literarischen Handschriften des Jacobitischen Markokloster in Jerusalem." *Oriens Christianus* Vol.2 1912: 317–338.

Beker, J.C. *Paul the Apostle, the Triumph of God in Life and Thought*. Edinburgh: T&T Clark, 1989.

Bermejo, L. *Paul, Missionary, Mystic, Martyr*. Anand: Gujrat Sahatiya Prakash, 2007.

Brock S.P., A. Butts, G. Kiraz, L. Van Rompay (editors) *Gorgias Encyclopaedic Dictionary* (Piscataway NJ: Gorgias Press, 2011).

——— "A Brief Outline of Syriac Literature." *Môrân 'Eth'ô*, Vol.9, 2009.

Bou Mansour, T. *Saint Paul dans la Patristique Syriaque*. Kaslik, 2010.

——— *La Théologie de Jacques de Saroug*. Kaslik: Vol.I, 1993; Vol. II, 2000.

Corbett, J.H. "The Pauline Tradition in Aphrahat." *Orientalia Christiana Analecta* 229 (1987)

Davies, W. D. *Paul and Rabbinic Judaism: Some Rabbinical Elements in Pauline Theology.* London: SPCK, 1948.

Dolabani, F.Y. *Catalogue of Syriac Manuscripts in St. Mark's Monastery.* Damascus, 1994.

Dunn, J. The *Theology of Paul the Apostle.* Michigan: W.B. Eerdmans Publishing Company, 2006.

Elliot, J.K. *The Acts of Paul in the Apocryphal New Testament.* Oxford: Clarendon Press, 1993.

―――― *The Apocalypse of Paul in the Apocryphal New Testament.* Oxford: Clarendon Press, 1993.

George, K.K. *Paul the Ambassador of Christ.* Thiruvalla, 1989.

Hansbury, M. "Love as an Exegetical Principle in Jacob of Serug," *The Harp* XXVII (2012): 353–68.

Kollamparampil, T. *Salvation According to Jacob of Serugh.* Bangalore: Dharmaram Publications, 2001.

Konat, J.A. *The Old Testament Types of Christ as Reflected in the Select Metrical Homilies (mimrē) of Jacob of Serugh.* Louvain-laNeuve, 1999.

Krüger, P. "Ein Missionsdokument aus früschristlicher Zeit." *Zeitschrift für Missionswissenschaft und Religionswissenschaft Heft* 4, 1958.

Macomber, W.F. "The Manuscripts of the Metrical Homilies of Narsai." *Orientalia Christiana Periodica* XXXIX, 1979.

Mathews, E.G., J.P. Amar, and K. McVey. St. Ephrem the Syrian, *Selected Prose Works: Commentary on Genesis, Commentary on Exodus, Homily on Our Lord, Letter to Publius.* Fathers of the Church 91. Washington, DC: Catholic University of America Press, 1994.

Murray, R. "Symbolism in Ephrem: The Theory of Symbolism in St. Ephrem's Theology." *Parole de l'Orient* 6,7 (1975–76): 1–20.

——— *Symbols of the Church and Kingdom.* Cambridge, 1975. (revised edition; London/Piscataway NJ, 2004).

Papoutsakis, M. "Formulaic Language in the Metrical Homilies of Jacob of Serugh." *Orientalia Christiana Analecta* 256 (1998): 445–451.

Parakkott, R. "St. Paul according to Jacob of Serugh." *The Harp* XXIII (2008): 41–46.

Sanders, J., C. A. Evans, ed. *Paul and the Scriptures of Israel* (Sheffield : JSOT Press, 1993).

Vööbus, A. "Handschriftliche Uberlieferung der Memre-Dichtung des Ja'qob von Serug." *CSCO* Vol.344 Subsidia Tomus 39. Louvain, 1973.

Wright, W. *A Short History of Syriac Literature.* Amsterdam: Philo Press, 1966.

Zibawi, M. "Les Syriens." *Orients chrétiens: entre Byzance et l'"Islam.* Paris: Desclée de Brouwer, 1995.

INDEX

BIBLICAL REFERENCES

Genesis
   4:18   61: 519
Exodus
   11:10   61: 525
Leviticus
   11:13–16   61: 37
Deuteronomy
   14:11–15   61: 37
I Kings
   19.8   61: 523
I Samuel
   13:20, 21   61: 25
Job
   39:26   61: 37
Psalms
   110:4   61: 519
Matthew
   10:16   61: 37; 62: 164
   22:39   62: 388
   27:60   61: 246
Mark
   12:31   62: 388
   15.46   61: 246
Luke
   4:22   61: 242
John
   19:42   61: 246
Acts
   7:58–8:1   62: 161
   8:3   61: 35
   9:1   61: 39
   9:4, 26   61: 23, 167
   9:4–5   61: 154, 177
   9:5a; 5b   61: 227, 228
   9:6   61: 363
   9:10–16   61: 434
   9:15   61: 24, 480; 62: 423
   9:16   61: 481
   9:17   61: 492
   9:18   61: 488
   9:21   61: 121
   9:25   62: 149
   9:26   61: 437
   14:12   62: 135
   14:13   62: 133
   14:19   62: 134, 152
   16:19–24   61: 23
   20:9–12   62: 142
   20:28   62: 221
   20:31   62: 279
   22:3   61: 41, 135
   22:5   61: 149
   22:6   61: 191
   22:7   61: 23, 154
   22:11   61: 177
   23:6   62: 146
   23:23–24:27 61: 23
   24:23,27   62: 33

26:10	61: 33	5:21	62: 355
26:13	61: 191	11:21–30	62: 15
26:14	61: 23	11:22	62: 154
26:15	61: 240	11:23–28	61: 23
26:24	62: 136	11:24	62: 33, 55
28:16–31	61: 23	11:25	62: 11, 56, 57

Romans

		11: 25–26	62: 10
6:6	61: 547	11:28	62: 33, 34
8:35	62: 314	12:2	61: 320;
8:38	62: 316		62: 63, 69
8:38–39	62: 320	12:4	62: 64
8:39	62: 318	12:7	61: 79
9:3	62: 301, 360	12:10	62: 17
9:4ff	62: 364		

Gal

9:33	62: 105	1:8–9	62: 263
11:1	62: 154	2:11	62: 263
11:33	62: 295	2:20	61: 540, 545, 593

1 Cor

1:22–23	62: 90, 105	6:14	61: 569, 585, 593
1:25	61: 98		
1:27	61: 75	6:17	62: 35, 43

Eph

2:2	62: 88	3:1	62: 31

Phil

3:9	61: 27	1:9	62: 31
3:10	61: 26–27	3:12	62: 228
4:4	62: 291	3:13	62: 234

Col

4:9	62: 123	1:23	62: 170
4:10	62: 166	1:24	62: 173
4:11	62: 130	2:16	61: 93

Thess

4:13	62: 153	1:9	62: 24

2 Tim

4:21	62: 151	4:2	62: 276
6:8,10	62: 138	4:7	62: 415
7:12	62: 271	4:8	62: 418

Hebrews

9:7	62: 27	5:6,10	61: 519
9:20a	62: 265	6:20	61: 519
9:20b	62: 266		
9:20–22	62: 267		
11:1	61: 512, 533		
15:31	62: 59		
15:32	62: 256		

2 Cor

7:10, 11, 15, 17	61: 519	11:5	61: 521

INDEX OF KEY TERMS

Abraham 62: 154, 363
Adam 62: 84
Adonai 61: 41, 71, 290
Ananias 61: 352, 434, 442, 447, 455, 482, 501
Anathema (accursed) 62: 306, 322, 346, 348, 356, 358, 360, 376, 384
Angels 61: 281, 331; 62: 122–23, 158, 263, 316, 323
Apostle 61: 67, 77, 191, 296, 306
Apostleship 61: 70, 557, 598; 62: 98
Arameans 62: 89–91, 104
Beauty 61: 128; 62: 46, 51, 78, 217, 223, 226, 251–259, 296, 403, 406
Cephas 62: 263
Christ 62: 90, 105, 115, 166, 175, 203, 228, 320, 373
Church 61: 13; 62: 176–78, 185, 188, 193, 202, 212, 215, 219
Colour 61: 470; 62: 75, 406
Corinth 62: 259
Covenant 62: 364, 367, 371
Cross 61: 102, 548, 565, 567, 578, 582–587; 62: 42, 60, 93–100, 107, 110–112, 164, 217
Crown 62: 414–424
Crucified 61: 13; 62: 36, 88, 90, 95, 583
Crucifixion 61: 3, 15, 96, 580; 62: 75, 378, 376

Curse 62: 306, 346, 348, 356, 358, 360, 376, 384
Disciples 61: 72, 74, 110, 118, 362, 364, 449, 454, 485, 497, 502; 62: 79, 85
Elijah 61: 523
Enoch 61: 521
Ephesus 62: 256
Eve 62: 83
Galatia 62: 258
Gentiles 61: 45
Golgotha 61: 270
Gospel 61: 97, 189, 303, 314, 465, 506; 62: 22–23, 25, 148, 230, 264, 414
Hermes 62: 135
Humility 61: 1, 159, 164, 173; 62: 67–78
Infirmity 62: 15, 16, 21
Inheritance 62: 368
Jerusalem 62: 260
Jesus 61: 1, 35, 40, 65, 116, 121, 145, 231, 301, 412, 491, 518, 532, 552; 62: 31, 43, 92, 159, 177, 181, 320, 355, 423.
Jew 61: 147, 280; 62: 55, 103, 265
Joseph 61: 242, 276
Judaism 61: 69, 87, 139
Law 61: 41, 142, 269, 298, 302; 62: 266, 370, 387
Learned 62: 413
Light 61: 189–218, 249, 400, 405, 486
Love 61: 57–63, 185; 62: 297–298, 308–359, 385–395

Lucid 61: 192
Majesty 61: 336, 341
Melchizedek 61: 519
Moses 61: 86, 95, 525; 62: 62
Mysteries 62: 62, 69, 77
Name 61: 108, 112, 229, 382, 480; 62: 96
Nation 61: 23, 45, 86, 123, 134, 189, 244, 266, 375; 62: 99
Nazarene 61: 67, 134, 238, 348
Nazareth 61: 116, 118–119, 228, 231, 234, 236, 328, 334
Overshadow 61: 204
Paradise 62: 64
Paul 61: 61, 64, 89, 103, 125, 190; 62: 107, 113, 119, 229, 247, 324, 345, 347, 358, 383, 389, 397, 401, 419
Persecuted 61: 23, 66, 76, 152, 156; 62: 130
Persecutor 61: 19, 23, 28, 57, 66, 78, 156, 222, 232, 436, 448; 62: 57, 123, 180
Peter 61: 101
Pharisees 61: 401; 62: 146
Praise 61: 255, 597; 62: 223, 285
Preach 61: 2, 481; 62: 22, 28, 90, 94, 100, 235, 262
Preacher 61: 314
Repentance 62: 381
Revelation 61: 191, 288, 295, 299, 320, 367, 575; 62: 61, 68, 72, 150

Roman 62: 145
Rome 62: 255
Sabbath 61: 47, 93, 268
Sadducees 61: 401
Saul 61: 25, 39, 54, 83, 114, 132, 154, 156, 163, 165, 197, 215, 225–229, 240, 324, 350, 365, 391, 415, 429, 438, 443, 447, 486, 489, 501
Scribe 61: 81, 401, 501
Sheol 61: 248, 275, 278
Simon 61: 81
Simplicity 61: 98, 464; 62: 111, 114
Son 61: 42, 197, 242, 306, 321; 62: 38, 192, 202, 208, 210, 219, 309 361, 380
Son of God 61: 117, 122, 232, 243 ; 62: 35, 76, 297, 357, 362
Spirit 62: 82; 269–74
Suffering 61: 13, 20, 379, 413; 62: 20, 36, 38, 47, 48, 50, 58, 118, 131, 167–220, 239, 240
Sun 61: 104, 188, 198, 205, 208; 62: 50, 118
Synagogues 61: 268
Syria 62: 257
Timothy 62: 275
Vessel 61: 24, 473, 479, 505; 62: 423
Zeal 61: 77, 141, 290, 377, 381, 387; 62: 161

www.ingramcontent.com/pod-product-compliance
Lightning Source LLC
Chambersburg PA
CBHW070739230426
43669CB00014B/2513